CLARTY STRANDS

A Walking Tour of the
Yorkshire Coast

by
Leonard Markham

With photographs
by Hugh Mayfield

HUTTON PRESS
1990

Published by the Hutton Press Ltd.
130 Canada Drive, Cherry Burton, Beverley
East Yorkshire HU17 7SB

Printed and bound by

Clifford Ward & Co. (Bridlington) Ltd.
55 West Street, Bridlington, East Yorkshire
YO15 3DZ

ISBN 0 907033 97 0

For Tom and Chloe

THE AUTHOR ...
that well known pedestrian.

CONTENTS

Page

INTRODUCTION

Compared with childhood experiences of industrial Leeds, my fleeting acquaintances with the Yorkshire coast were high adventure — wild headlands, precipitous cliffs, sands, reefs, wrecks, smugglers' coves, and a romantic and sometimes barbarous history to delight the most bloodthirsty of boys.

Since boyhood, I have held a cherished ambition to walk every inch of the area, recording my impressions and experiences in a book. This volume, spiked with more than a dash of Yorkshire humour, is that ambition fulfilled.

A traditionalist even in youth, I have always been a vocal champion of walking — a conditioner of limbs, restorer of appetites and soother of minds afflicted by frenetic modern living. Today I am positively strident in its praise. Known in motoring circles as 'that well known pedestrian', I tramp happily on my way, obeying only the eclectic helm of curiosity, unencumbered by thoughts of depreciation, congestion and the excrutiating problems of parking. Don those idling boots and join me along the clarty strands.

Len Markham
March 1990

AUTHOR'S NOTES

The history of the Yorkshire coast has been affected by events both insidious and cataclysmic. Marauding Romans and Vikings have left their marks, but in 1974 a treachery more odious and profound than all foreign invasions afflicted the area. At an administrative stroke, Local Government Reorganisation redefined county boundaries, imposing the new county names of Humberside, North Yorkshire and Cleveland on an almost universally resistant population. The new names, as recent events are showing will be short lived, but in any event, for the purposes of this book I will raise my colours for the names I know and love best. For me, the coastline from Spurn to Middlesbrough will always be in Yorkshire, despite all the bureaucratic meddlings.

A brief word on practicalities. For the most part, Yorkshire's coastal terrain is rugged, and its weather, even in high Summer, can be foul and unpredictable. So set out well equipped, with sturdy boots, warm and ample clothing, waterproofs and elastoplast!

As far as seeking a couch for the night is concerned, if you are anything like me, (a Yorkshireman: by definition a Scotsman with the generosity squeezed out) attempt to economise by staying with relatives and friends. Unfortunately, even for me, this was not always possible, and, on occasions, reluctantly, I had to unzip my pockets and abscind brass. The venues for the amputations are given, along with details of other recommended fee-paying establishments, in the Appendix.

> "He who is indeed of the brotherhood does not voyage in quest of the picturesque, but of certain jolly humours."

Robert Louis Stevenson

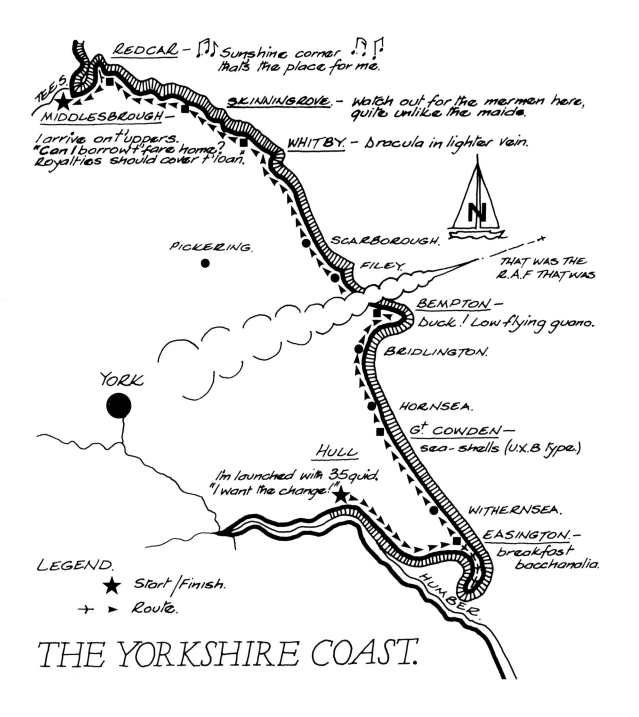

THE YORKSHIRE COAST.

Hull
Paull
Easington

Although Yorkshire's principal port embraces the Humber rather than the North Sea, its character has been so much shaped by the sea that it deserves mention in any coastal guide. And it is there, in the Old Town, an area formerly delineated by the rivers Hull and Humber, and a defensive moat that was dug to link the two watercourses in 1321, that my coastal journey begins.

Until 1980 I set not a foot in Hull, but all that changed following a night out with a fish merchant's daughter. Testing my suitability for betrothal, her father whisked me from my bed at 5 o'clock one raw December morning to introduce me to the delights of the fish dock. My brief encounter with a filleting knife and several limp haddock was not an unmitigated disaster. I managed to retain several fingers, and I married the girl in the end.

Since my marriage I have thoroughly explored this busy port, rejoicing in its wonderful blend of old with new. Where in the county is there such harmony of ancient spires, intimate alleys, refurbished docks and warehouses and the bold vibrant architecture of the 1990's? Not in York, that museumed city in aspic; certainly not in unlovely Leeds whose redevelopment is, in comparison, stolid and discordant. Yet here in Hull, a city that has endured bombing, the near catastrophes of benighted town planners and the grinding recession of its fishing industry, is integration supreme, crowned by the engineering marvel of the age — a symbol of renaissance which struts across the Humber as bold as brass — theBridge — the longest single span structure of its kind in the world.

Strategically sited at the confluence of the Hull and the estuarine Humber, Hull was established by the monks of Meaux Abbey, whose enterprise received royal patronage in 1299. King Edward I coveted Hull as an ideal replacement for nearby Ravenser, a fast disappearing port, prostrate to the sea after centuries of erosion. Under his royal charter, growth of the newly appointed Kingston (King's Town)-on-Hull was rapid. Quays and defences were built, a ferry link was established with Lincolnshire, and, as trade flourished, Hull rose to national and international prominence.

Between the 14th and 18th centuries the town expanded as a port, a religious centre, and as a military and naval base, protected by a citadel, block houses, batteries of guns and an encircling arc of fortifications which withstood twin royalist sieges during the Civil War. Until the 18th century, development was contained within the ancient boundaries, but the impetus of the Industrial Revolution led to urban expansion, the loss of important medieval buildings, and the construction of 7 deep water docks straddling the lines of fortifications to the north and west.

The bounteous sea stimulated further expansion when the adventurous pursuit of the whale began in 1765. For a century the distant slaughter brought great wealth to the port, but the increasing scarcity of the most persecuted of creatures stimulated the growth of trawling. For over 120 years a seemingly inexhaustible harvest of fish was the mainstay of the local economy. Then came the infamous Cod Wars and the withdrawl of the fleet. As a stunned newcomer I will forever remember the melancholy sight, an armada of rusting hulks, redundant reapers of the shoals, destined by the politics of the sea for the breaker's yard.

By 1980 the scaly tide had ebbed to an Icelandic trickle, and the "Silver Cod", a trophy once awarded annually to the most successful trawler skipper, took its superannuated place alongside generations of reluctant landlubbers. But today, with vision and initiative,

9

spurred by local authority, governmental and EC grants, Hull's phoenix has taken confident wing, soaring achievements like the riverside and marina developments receiving national acclaim. So what better way to begin than by enjoying Hull's new found fame? What better place to embark than on the banks of the eponymous river below Drypool Bridge, where 800 years ago development first began?

I set out posh shod for a city amble, as excited as fictional hero Robinson Crusoe, who departed from this very spot in 1651. I walked the planks which form a stout riverside promenade, built totally in keeping with a 'workaday river' humming with sea-drones — dredgers, flaky paint coasters and grubby barges by the swarm. Framing this timeless scene is the Tidal Surge Barrier. If architectural and technological integration is a hallmark of Hull's resurgence, the harmonious design of this recently commissioned wizardry is a pinnacle achievement. Its boom, intended to prevent the hitherto frequent inundations of the old harbour, is lowered with great effect at high tide...but only if the operator keeps awake. Yes, the lad has been known to nod off!

Behind, and running parallel to the riverside, is the oldest, and perhaps the most interesting street in Hull. Narrow, cobbled High Street, its storied gables sprouting hoists, pulleys and the hardware of a mercantile past, is the perfect setting for three of Hull's premier museums. Having illicitly slaked a thirst in the magnificent panelled bar of the Ye Olde Black Boy Inn — a notorious rendezvous for slavers in the days before emancipation — I inspected the crammed displays in the Archaeological, Transport and Wilberforce House museums. The former home of the famous slavery abolitionist William Wilberforce, is a provocative memory to one of the most inspirational MP's who ever graced the House of Commons. I left the chilling sight of manacles and whips with the campain slogan of the abolitionists ringing in my ears ... 'am I not a man and a brother', heading for the largest parish church in England to give grateful thanks for the freedom to stride on.

An unconventional Christian, I saw through the bunkem of inter-denominational rivalry and allegiance to divisive dogma and symbolism years ago. As with my wanderings, so with my churchgoing. Entering Holy Trinity for the first time I felt I belonged.

Guidebooks usually extol at tedious length the architectural and historical merits of churches. The average reader is bored rigid. Over the centuries, what were centres for both spiritual and social activities have become, to some extent, fossilized mausoleums, sepulchres for increasingly irrelevant ideals. There is too much emphasis on heritage and addiction to ancient rote and creed. Churches must adapt and attract a wider community. Alienate ordinary people and these monuments in figured stone will crumble, but for the unheralded lifeblood toil of parishioners like those of Holy Trinity. Insignificant, dwarfed by capitals and soaring arches, are the flowers of their devotion — hassocks, simple in form, magnificently intricate in design and detail, depicting in a myriad embroidered threads every aspect of Hull life.

Lingering in the shadows of the church, and the old red-bricked Grammar School, where Andrew Marvell, the celebrated patriot and satirist was taught, I sniffed the early morning air. Undigested, a rasher or two grumbled as a smell assailed my nose, tweeking it along to a confrontation of the senses. Hot, golden, and scrumptious, the assailant had his compulsive way, and I found myself devouring a pavement feast of fish and chips. The assault on county appetites is waged by Bob Carver whose institutional ranges occupied a favoured pitch in Market Square until hygiene regulations forced his business indoors. Continuing queues tell the capitulary tale.

Disposing of the evidence of this superfluous intake of calories (I resolved to walk hard in the weeks ahead) I headed for the Town Docks Museum, a tribute to Hull's maritime past, packed to the gunwales with exhibits. Embodied in pictorial displays, tableaux, and an armada

HULL MARINA ... perfect compliment to woolly vested yachtsmen.

11

of model ships, I saw the pride of this great seafaring city, learning something of the absorbing but gruesome history of the whaling industry, the hideous tools of this bloody trade striking a melancholy and repugnant chord, pitched into even darker discordancy by a background lament of cetacean sonar. The lament for the trawling industry, which in 1960 employed almost 3000 men, is muted. The most dangerous occupation in Britain, claiming 99 deaths in 1955 alone was, and remains, an unsung trade. Next time I'm splashing on the vinegar I'll chew on this... 'however bravely man may brag of his science and skill, and however much in a flattering future, that science and skill may augment, yet for ever and for ever, to the crack of doom, the sea will insult and murder him, and pulversise the stateliest, stiffest frigate he can make... ' (Herman Melville: Moby Dock).

'Enough of museums!' complained my itchy feet, hankering for the open road. Denying them full throttle, I ambled towards the Marina.

To woolly vested Yorkshiremen like me, the word conjures an image of sleek vessels, sophistication and sun, and although the wherewithal for a decktop tan is generally denied, Hull's marina can compete with any tropical climes. Occupying the site of two former docks, it offers an anchorage of practical and strikingly visual appeal.

In creating the facility, newly enclosed by vibrant brickwork and garlands of stout chains, the authorities have taken great pains to conserve the rugged dockland character, retaining mellow stonework, refurbishing warehouses, bollards and bridges, and restoring for public inspection the still bullish Spurn Lightship, the first in a historic collection of vessels celebrating Hull's maritime past. Set against a distant city-scape of domes and towers, here is the perfect compliment to the yachtsmen of the northern seas. In any age there has never been anything lily-livered about Hull's seafarers, and dockland architecture has always reflected their virility. In the marina, tradition lives on.

Fattened up for the fray by the mother-in-law, next day I slipped the Old Town anchor, crossing the Hull and marching eastwards into the sea-girt granary of Holderness, an area as remote as many a Highland glen.

Ideally, my route should have companioned the shore, but dockland sprawl diverted me onto the A1033. Once a track for pole-wagons, Hedon Road gave up its rustic ghost to the motor vehicle years ago, its verge side pastures and windmills swept away by houses, factories, shops, docks, a hospital, a prison and a monstrous chemical works, a visual and nasal foretaste of the eternal stoke-hole guaranteed to keep any walker on the straight and narrow. And so with my oblivious head down, for once I yomped along, using the four 'sea-trial' miles to Paull roundabout to flex the limbs for the more pleasant leagues ahead, breathing not too deeply as I hurried past the smoke and flames of the sprawling works.

Resisting the lure of the 'King of Holderness' — the beacon church of the ancient port of Hedon — I turned right, pinching my nose for a few yards yet. Relieved at last, I sniffed the freshening breeze of Paull, striding down a langouress main street extravagant with a flush of inns. With tainted palate I made for the Humber Tavern for a mouth-wash of excellent Yorkshire ale — a venerable draught, typically tangy and energising with its hallmark halo like clotted cream.

I sat alone in the bar, sipping, watching through the window as a vast tanker laboured towards the infernal works with its cargo of crude. It was balmy May, but mysteriously the landlord entered and lit a roaring fire... for whom? Agued, wizened, sea-drained by a hundred blows the inheritor of the hearth shuffled in for his daily dram, brought by an acolyte waiter without a word. The old man was silent for a while, then for a wet of his garrulous whistle this veteran of the Arctic convoys waxed nostalgic about his retirement home, residential, nondescript, quiet and forgotten, fading from the acme of its pugnacious past, decommissioned to impotency since the glory days of its man-of-war shipyard and 19 gun battery that protected the river road to Hull in 1864.

Save for the buffeting wind, the martial airs have gone. Puall lingers on in domesticity. Leaving the man to his consolation malt I headed off into the wind.

The estuarine path leads south to Spurn, past a residentially converted former lighthouse of 1836 and the still quaint Anson Cottages not a wave's leap from the shore. From the path, the gimballed eye is drawn back along the waves to Hull, and across to the port of Immingham on the Humber's distant bank. Diluting its industrialisation in a swirl of blank horizons — a torment for agrophobics — the Humber is a conglomerate flow, a dozen rivers mingling with the waters of the North Sea in constant flux.

The battle against erosion, a fact of precarious life along the entire coast, is waged in Paull by a modern concrete wall. Below the path I found earlier attempts at containment of both the river and potential invaders —regimented rows of remnant stockades — a littoral Flanders Field of gnawed and nibbled timbers draped with wrack and weed.

A casual survey reveals little other evidence of fortified Paull, but following the high ground I chanced upon a steep ditch, the very heart of the defences overgrown with shrubs. Bumping down I peered up at a brick curtain wall pierced by gun slits, silent embrasures colonised by birds and windowed by gossamer threads. Pushing through the scrub, I examined yard upon yard of still perfect bonding musing on the prodigality of war. Emerging into the sunshine I stumbled across a World War II pillbox; folly upon defensive folly, stratified testimony to our perennial belligerency.

The Thorngumbald Lights, as with their delightful name, stick out like sore, yet benevolent metal thumbs, guiding shipping away from the treacherous Paull Holme Sands. One white, the other a post-box red pulsating then against an eye-stabbing background of oil-seed rape, they stand alongside the aptly named Waterguard Cottage, a lonely keeper's house protected by a brute of an Alsatian. Aware of my bare and appetising ankles, I inched cautiously along the narrow crossing over a drain.

A trio of schoolboy anglers ledgered on, peering down into a disgusting broth of sewage unconcerned at my plight. Prepared for instant flight I ventured on, staring hypnotically into covetous canine eyes that betrayed a sweet-toothed passion for rambler on the hoof. Unfortunately for the dog a fence intervened. 'Goodness gracious!' I exclaimed. 'Good Boy', I whimpered, quitting the scene and resolving never to be a postman.

If you need to be alone walk on, wallow in the sea of contemplation, absorb the emollient miles. Apart from the distinctive Paull Holme Watchtower, a well preserved brick-built lookout erected by monks, and the seeping mudflats, there is little to distract your introspection until you come to Stone Creek. All this might change, however, if a mooted tidal barrage is ever built.

The subject of an ongoing feasibility study, the ambitious two option scheme would provide either a 4½ mile barrage from a point south-east of Cleethorpes to Spurn Head, or a shorter, nearly 3 miles alternative scheme, west from Killingholme marshes to a point north of Stone Creek. Harnessing tidal power, the barrages would generate electricity, create leisure and tourism opportunities, assist flood protection and improve facilities for shipping, as well as providing several thousand short-term construction jobs. On the negative side environmentalists contend that both schemes would be ecological disasters, resulting in an enormous loss of tidal feeding habitats for nearly 100,000 birds. I am an old stick-in-the-mud on such controversies, a disciple to the doctrine of 'rendering to the birds what is the birds'.

I saw very few fowl on my way to Stone Creek. Fed by several drains, this brown curdled sump offers a meagre haven to the local yacht club. A bridge, a trio of lonely farmsteads and long distance views of the steeples of Ottringham and Patrington churches complete the inventory.

In terms of acreage, inventories have burgeoned in these parts over the years, the result of land reclamation on a grand scale. Curtseying, I passed a Crown Estate

STONE CREEK ... a brown curdled sump.

Commissioners' signboard proclaiming HM's sovereignty over Sunk Island, formerly a morass of muddy creeks and tide-washed sandbanks reclaimed by Cornelius Vermuyden and his followers to provide over 10,000 acres of the most fertile of land. Tug those hems of ermine and you can, at a price, engage in wild-fowling here, but a royal largesse, the so called 'courtesy path', can be enjoyed absolutely free.

Near Hawkins Point the Humber's south bank commands attention. Hawkins hey... a name to shiver the timbers. Ahoy there! A vast yer swabs! Give him a broadside matey! Er, pardon me. Dad and Uncle were Jack Tars, (Her Majesty's Ships *Implacable* and *Valiant*) and I have never quite got over Treasure Island. Back to Hawkins Point. Take your spy-glass and you can see, near Immingham, an odd looking tower: perhaps a minaret or campanile, or just a plain old chimney?

Another good hour saw me on the site of Burstall Priory at Skeffling Clough. As near as I can fathom, Clough is synonymous with sluice, and there are sluices galore in a district still shedding its submarine past. High and dry, the little but spacious church of St. Helen's is easily visible from the path, as are the patient silhouettes of large ships anchored in Grimsby Road. I spent some time pressed to the glass like a U-boat captain. Suddenly I noticed a looming sandbar — tomorrow's target — Spurn Head.

Having stomped 25 long miles since leaving Hull, I arrived in Easington blistered and tuckered out, anxiously seeking accommodation as the bats in the belfry of All Saint's began to stir. I stopped a man in dubious charge of a wheel-barrow to ask advice. He looked me up and down and sniffed copious amount of snuff slowly into each flaccid nostril. Then he scratched his chin. 'Aye' he said at last. 'Tha looks proper buggered lad. Well I can tell thee. As far as Easington digs is concerned tha's three selections. There's rough uns, middle uns and wine with everything uns, depending on how much tha wants to pay'. As it was my birthday, and being financially allergic to the grape, I knocked on the door of the 'middle un', dreading the apparition of a Valkerie, a transmuted landlady who is known to terrorise those parts. My apprehension melted at the sight — a Yorkshire belle, fond and friendly, a mound of bonny plumpness who whisked me off to bed in a trice.

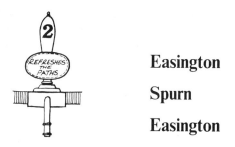

Easington

Spurn

Easington

Aroused from a luscious sleep by wafts of bacon, I took my place at table alongside a burly Geordie from Easington's Gas Terminal, a storage and distribution facility that shattered the rural idyll in 1967. "That'll put lead in your pencil bonny lad", chuckled Geordie, watching as my breakfast was hauled in on a sled. Never have cholesterol or poly-saturated fats been more abundantly or appetisingly presented. There was a constellation of eggs, succulent sausages, hatchet sliced ham, mushrooms, tomatoes, a devil of a kidney, a cob of black pudding, toast, and a cauldron of black tea, steaming in a samovar salvaged from a local wreck. 'We likes to see you have a good start to the day' said the great provider. Start? After that lot, I needed jump leads!

It was a morning for idling. His Fiery Highness, a sphere as rare as UFO's in Holderness, beat down. I wallowed in the heat and wandered, examining the commodious village square and a row of houses surmounted by a look-out tower. Easington is hushed by a muted drone, at first a noise, an imposition, precipitously blamed on the Gas Terminal. Realisation dawns. I recognised the sound of the tide and heard no more.

A hive of self-sufficiency, an old fishing community remote and undisturbed until the gasmen called, Easington is quiet despite the intrusion, its sea-cobbled snugness crowned by the 11th century church of All Saint's. Near the church is a remarkably preserved 14th century barn, a designated ancient monument that sets the medieval scene for a fragrant tribute to Shakespeare. Scenting the old timbers is a pungent garden inspired by the lines from a dozen plays. Never has labelling been more eloquent. ' ... I know a bank where the wild thyme blows... ' (Midsummer Nights Dream); 'he plays at quoits well and eats conger and fennel...' (Henry IV); 'and skrieks like mandrakes torn out of the earth' (Romeo and Juliet). I found the poetic gardener about his weeding.

He showed me his cottage. Fronting the path, it is plain and unpretentious, perhaps deliberately so, concealing at the rear a vision of Old England that would have had the bard scurrying for his quill. Bordered by bright flowers is a limpid pond crammed with red rudd, flashing darts of vermilion answering their master's call like pet hounds. I loitered for a while, before setting out with vigour on the lonely track to Spurn.

The sight did my economic heart good. A man approached carefully guiding a bicycle ladened with timber, bath-scum of the tide, a briny dowry of broken spars, decking, oars, flag poles and fish boxes, all neatly tied with string. I nodded and past on by.

Greeting the Humber for the last time, I stepped out alongside desolate mudflats to Kilnsea. Erosion is the omnipotent reality, the eternal threat to Kilnsea and a score of other villages along the coast, A cowering shadow of its former self, Kilnsea ekes out a meagre existence, pincered by the twin assaults of river and sea. Bows agape, three pitiful hulks on the Humber strand gasped resignation. Like a kindred tramp 150 years before me I found the berth of melancholia. Sir George Head lamented the plight of the old church in 1835... 'in one large mound lay the ruins, large masses of the walls adhering closely cemented together, as well as fragments of the round spire, the latest avalanches of earth consisting of rich churchyard mould, in which were profusely scattered bones, skulls, and fragments of coffins... ' Those very bones have been powdered away. Nothing of that devastation remains. The replacement church built in 1864 awaits its appointed hour.

EASINGTON –
ALL SAINTS ...
it crowns the sea-cobbled
snugness.

KILNSEA ... well and truly anchored.

Scanning the horizon slamming flow, mindful of the fate of other local villages, I was moved to rare verse:

Gnawed, eroded, clawed,
Tide-smashed, immersed, dispersed,
Ground to sandy anonymity.
Submerged, plunged, the indelible past
   expunged,
Nibbling, the vandalising splash engulfed
   without distinction.
Gone the guiding flame. Snuffed out.
Undermining, yard by tumbling yard,
Devouring, scouring, the retreating home-
   steads cowering.
Groins and gabions, bulwark mounds,
   their feeble challenge bursted.
Prostrate, abandoned, braced, the wrathful
   surge accursed.
Spindrift scythe, North Wind honed, its
   cohorts full blown,
A vengeful harvest mown.
Old Kilnsea, Orwithfleet, Sunthorp, Raven-
   spurn, Ravenserodd,
All levelled, absorbed,
Rendered by the pulverising force to
   Spurn's accretion.
Lapping, the eternal wash assuages.
Blank horizons; forgetfulness consorting in
   final erasure.

In former years such erosion was put to grim advantage. In 1770 a murderer was clasped with iron hoops and swung from a gibbet at Hornsea, until the ornament was washed away.

I wandered on bamboozled by the mirage — the shimmering arc of distant Spurn aping the southern shore. The trek to the point proved a blister too far.

A nature reserve controlled by the Yorkshire Naturalists' Trust, Spurn is one of the most notable sand and shingle pits in the country, an ecological niche for a kaleidoscope of plants, animals and birds. Formed bydeposits scoured from the Holderness coast, Spurn is constantly being enlarged, although records show that about every 250 years the peninsula neck is breached by the sea, the whole conglomeration being swept away,only to be reinstated some distance to the west.

Treading in the still damp wake of a recent breach, I saw the makeshift repair, everything and the kitchen sink having been enlisted to stem the tide. Broken lamp standards have their uses.

The road arrows on, flanked by swathes of uncommon sea-buckthorn, an attractive shrub whose bright orange berries are coveted by migrating birds. I felt somewhat precarious, a pirate walking an uncertain plank, wondering about that repair and whether I might enjoy the Crusoe life. Spinning on my heels at the sound, I confronted an imaginary lorry... only the engine of the waves, racing and malevolent on the seaward side, idling on placid Humber.

Knitted with marram grass, the great spit hosts an unusual community of specialised plants including the striking sea-bindweed and sea-holly. Colourful pyramidal orchids, storksbill, yellow-wort, restharrow and common centaury decorate the dunes. Bird life is varied and abundant, binocular sore spotters, converging for fleeting peeks at such rarities as the thrust nightingale, blue throat and golden oriole, as well as the more common oystercatcher, curlew, dunlin and mallard. Stopping frequently I watched curlews probing for lunch and turnstones about their revelations. The elusive point seemed to retreat in the haze.

Over an hour's hard slog delivered me to Spurn's 519,000 candle-power lighthouse. Built in 1895, at 120′ it soars above the sea, emitting a flash every 15 seconds. The light is visible for up to 17 miles. Only feet from the tower is a curious circular compound, the site of a 90′ coalfired predecessor lighthouse completed in 1779 by John Smeaton the famous Leeds engineer. The old light was pulled down and pressed into erosion service in 1895. Sprouting from the Humber mud is the last of a number of secondary lighthouses built to complement Smeaton's great work. Latterly used as a magazine for explosives, it

NEXT TO GO ...
to sandy anonymity.

20

SPURN ... its use and abuse has been as regular as the tide.

is now a perch for grateful cormorants.

Use and abuse of Spurn has been as regular as the tide ever since the monk Wilgils built his cell at the lonely tip in 670 AD. Militarisation from the Napoleonic and Great Wars has left its scars. A labryinth of pill-boxes and ordnance platforms desecrate the monastic solitude. The big guns have gone; scrapped, rusted away. Feet thick concrete defies the years. But what of the modern complex? The new pilot jetty and the coast-guard observation tower are thoroughly practical, and in a coastal context, unobtrusive. In comparison, the replacement lifeboat houses are an aberration. Residential transplants from some inner city, they are an incongruous disaster. But the lifeboat station, one of only three in the country manned by a full time crew, redeems the noble spirit of Spurn. Jutting out boldly from the sand, even in the calm of a May afternoon it was inspirational, an insubstantial shed restraining *City of Bradford II*, her and her sister boats the pinnacle morality of our bulldog breed. Watching a convoy of ships awaiting the buzz of the pilot, I thought about gale lashed nights mid-Winter, and about May-days of the desperate kind. Would I be a lifeboat man? Not for all the tea in China.

About faced I stepped out for Middlesbrough.

Inevitably the first of many thousands of east coast caravans blotted the view. They settle like regimented locusts, seeking a perverse solitude. Huddled yet strangely aloof they disgorge their contemplative souls who, year by year, jack-up their homes and regress from the crumbling shore. I trod warily around slabby hardstandings and an abandoned paddling pool cantilevered over the debris of fresh falls. For some, here is grand communion. For others the mauling sea nags at relaxation.

Leading to the scene of my early morning encounter with a near bulging death, the path skirts Easington Lagoons, an Area of Special Protection afforded to visiting little terns. Only swans plied the mirrored surface, 27 flagships of an incomparable line, gloaming etched shadows hushing the close of day.

My landlady's greeting was as effusive as her breakfast, and her skill with pin and plaster a mighty comfort to maltreated feet. Repaired, I hobbled off to the Neptune for a spell of well earned immobility. Drowning in my own ale whilst under the influence of sleep was a distinct possibility, so I slithered off to bed.

Easington

Aldbrough

Hornsea

I feigned lock-jaw and had a liquid breakfast, but no amount of wriggling could evade the valedictory kiss. It kept me going for miles.

Bocking at the smell, I followed a rashered trail through Easington's caravan park which boasts a camp store and a modern swimming pool. Brighter than most, the park cocks a jaunty snook at the North Sea in an illusion of permanency. In utter disdain of the sea I discovered a lone camper braving the swell in a costume that would have suited Prince Albert. 'Our Perce swears by his early morning dip', said a jolly towel-bearer buttoned to the chin.

Giving the Gas Terminal a wide berth, I followed the shore, basking in the enervating emptiness. Four days out and I had finally cast the sedentary yoke, all stiffness had gone and I bounded along gulping the tonic-wine of a breeze, fancying on reaching Middlesbrough by nightfall.

From his cab, the bulldozer driver gave me a puzzled wave. Visitors in anything but hard-hats are unusual on pipe-end beach, where the constant reinstatement of tide-washed sand safeguards the precarious investment of Amoco and BP. Sheet piling gives crude additional protection to the pipeline as it snakes the cliffs. The coast from Bridlington to the Humber is being eroded at the rate of 2 metres per annum, and expediency necessarily deploys an instant but motley assortment of coast defences. Long term the answer may lie in confronting attrition tide on, developing proposals for the construction of energy absorbing artificial reefs offshore. The boffins are currently beavering away with mathematical models and simulations based on the use of spent tyres and up to 500 million tons of colliery spoil from the Yorkshire and Durham coalfields. The theory promises a reduction in erosion by up to 50%. For the present, Winter and Spring storms will continue their offensives unchallenged, engulfing the mean and the makeshift.

I detest litter. The accumulations below Dimlington, the highest point on the Holderness coast, are dispiriting. One man's rubbish is a communal eyesore, the insulted eye conjuring a mighty conflagration. I trudged through fish boxes, ravaged nets, oil barrels, tin-cans, light bulbs, a charnel-house of splintered timbers, and a bio-perennial nightmare of assorted plastic. Whatever happened to the romantic spoil of the beachcomber? It endureth yet. The lilting chords of an ancient mariner muffled the tide, and amongst the heaps I found a lyrical bottle, its message strangely prominent through the surf-spewed glass. 'I wonder where it will be?' said the crumpled business card, redolent of salt and cheap wine.

I wrote to the consignor, the captain of the good ship *Volvox Delta*, a dredger engaged in trenching North Sea gas pipes. 'We were all in good states!' he replied. 'I do this in the seclusion of my cabin, and I wish the bottle good luck. When I launched him, I wished him well and wondered if anybody really cared about a bottle today?'

Near Holmpton, I found calving glaciers of till shearing from the unstable and menacing cliff. Death knelled, the tragically named Cliff House Farm has been abandoned to its fate. The village of Holmpton, a confident distance from the shore, in contrast, breathes repose. In luscious torpor I floated down the lane, a May flushed inebriate. If silence is golden, the murmur of an English Spring is a midal roar, intoxicating the senses. Exploiting my daze a bridal path tugged me off to North Farm.

Before their subjugation, farms hummed to the rhythm of the seasons. Once cajoled now enslaved, they groan discordancy, yielding wasteful abundancy in their

SURF-SPEWED GLASS ... message in a bottle.

thrall to high-tech and agro-chemicals. But the owner of North Farm cherishes simpler days, relishing his Arcadia. Triumphs of self-sufficiency, he preserves a dovecote and an ancient stew pond, alongside a beautifully extended farmhouse, bedecked with flowers, the bower echoing the joy of an emigré author from the south who came to Holmpton in 1896. Stuffed with approbation and irreverent jollity 'A Cockney in Arcadia' by H.A. Spurr captures the spirit of the place. Only the names have been changed to protect the comical. 'He is not yet 4 but he is in knickerbockers. Whilst in — ahem! — feminine bondage, he was I suspect a little uncertain as to his age; but now that he is no longer a human tadpole, having as it were, outgrown his tail, he answers any question on the subject with the aggressive, almost threatening assertion, 'I'm a boy!'... a publican portly and prosperous whose barbarous opulence sunned itself in his glossy whiskers and wealth of waist...' 'If you drive Ruddiman's trap you will find out one or two amusing things. The horse firstly stops whenever you cry 'good morning', to any one. Secondly it stops at a certain pub in Patrick's Town, and lastly at the station. This gives you as good an idea of Ruddiman as you can want'.

Pushing on for Withernsea, I passed a gentleman. He was hand-feeding blue-tits. Arcadia indeed.

The companionship of a child brings an impish naïveté to seaside tramps. An excuse for hair down pranks, a day visitor, my young son Tom, led the way, skipping along with his wooden gun. He found a deep ditch, The Runnel, where a rakish pill-box provided the perfect ambuscade. With only minor flesh wounds, we hit the beach.

The pack straps parted before I had travelled a further mile. The magpie proclivities of enquiring children should be enouraged, but ten pounds of souvenir pebbles is perhaps a trifle excessive. Furtively I discarded the load and led the search for Neptune's treasure — abandoned 'sea toys'. Passing an awful Stalag Luft VII collection of chalets we marched into Withernsea, our free bucketsand spades at the ready. The beach was deserted.

Utterly devoid of picturesqueness, Withernsea has declined as a seaside resort since its railway closed in 1964. The town is dominated by a handsome, butrecently redundant, lighthouse of 1894, prudently set back amongst residential streets several hundred yards from the stoutly defended shore. Apart from the lighthouse, a castellated gateway that led to a long since vanished pier, and rows of smart houses smug behind their sea wall, amorphous Withernsea is architecturally depressing. And yet, as with countless resorts throughout the country, in season, it is for some the holiday ideal, a mixture of sandy simplicity, indulgence and coin-operated fun. The beach was empty but the arcades were thronged.

Extricating myself from the sand, I said cheerio to the trainee grave digger and set the compass for Aldbrough, passing another gentleman along the way. I am compelled to recall the sight. A removal man, his sign painted on the side of a rickety wheelbarrow, sweated above a precarious stack of furniture. I hoped his client had not bought the lighthouse.

The villages of Old Withernsea, Newsham, Owthorne, Waxholme, Sand Le Mere, Monkwike, Monkwell, and Ringborough have been wiped off the map. In the next seven miles I found not a trace. Nostalgic and defiant, the retention of the old names on farm and field is all that remains. Printed on the OS map the word 'Waxholme' is next for expunction. I examined the old farmstead with its gaunt punctured buildings and rusting heaps of machinery. Amidst the jumble were 105mm howitzer shell boxes empty of the ammunition made for an enemy who thankfully never came.

Above Waxholme an appendage of the village of Tunstall marrs the landscape. As caravan parks go, Sandley Mere with its fishing lake, shops, amusements

WITHERNSEA PIER ... nobbut a gate.

and club, is very desirable for the gregarious tin-canners, but for those who appreciate the natural order of things, the puzzling vision of four blue minarets lauding it above the trees, is the limit. Before I got near enough to discern the wobbling reality, a local explained, 'It's one of those flaming blow-up bouncy things for kids, with four tit-ends on top'.

The path at Monkwith has been clawed away. Sliced from the cliffs, tettering slabs of farmland sprout unreapable crops. Walking near the edge became dangerous. Reluctantly I trod the corn.

Admiral Storr's Tower near the village of Hilston was built in 1750 as a landmark for sailors. It served me well in descending mist, pinpointing my position, guiding me towards the settlements of Grimston and Grimston Garth, a charming Georgian-Gothic mansion built for Thomas Grimston by the famous Yorkshire architect John Carr in 1786. Dynastic founder, Sylvester-de-Grymston was granted the cliff top spoils by William the Conqueror, following valorous service at Hastings in 1066. Commissioned to replace the moated family seat that was burned down around 1700, Grimston Garth was spared no expense. Always imperious, yet now demurely closeted by tall trees, the castellated, three-towered extravagance was intended as a luxurious summer retreat, the pantry order books telling an indulgent tale. Determined to protect his home against Napoleonic designs, Thomas raised, at his own expense, the stalwart Grimston Yeomanry. The booted duke returned them to their ploughs.

From Beacon Hill, the tower at Ringborough assumes a medieval guise. Closer inspection reveals a crumbling World War II look-out station surrounded by ancillary dereliction and rank weeds that hide a commando course of a path.

I negotiated a deep concrete channel throbbing a brown stooly crud. One slip in my attempted crossing and I would have been quarantined. My fine tweeds would have been condemned to the flame. Whistling an anodyne snatch from 'Everything's Coming Up Roses' I relievedly reached the end of the plank, but the praise-be's were premature. The Odysseyan trial was just beginning.

'If it's sporting a pair of danglers, run'. The sage advice of my old grandpappy surged to mind, and I was onestride ahead of the bull all the way to the electric fence, until the twin shocks of current and horn propelled me through the air. I hit the ground and tumbled, returning to the coastal path from which I so foolishly erred. Limping into the pleasant village of Aldbrough, I sought out the Star and Garter and bathed my wounds.

Next morning I was joined by a photographer chum, a whizz with the lens and a sterling man to have around when elastoplasting nether regions. Surgery complete, we swung our sacks and set out for the local church.

Like-minded walking companions are a boon. Nonchalant of horn and endless hoofing, with encouraging quips, they render even rainy days bright, and extra pairs of eyes and hands are always useful —musically so, when your pal, like mine, happens to be one of the finest organ players in the North of England. Not that we stumbled across many Würlitzers on our cliff top stomp, although churchy reeds sprout thick on the Yorkshire coast, giving frequent opportunities for symphonic appreciations of the clarty strands. Our breakfast time renditions of Wagner's *Flying Dutchman* have had sextons lurching in the aisles!

The door of Aldbrough's 13th century church of St. Bartholomew was locked, so we improvised, rollicking along belly-spasmed in song.

The Ministry of Defence soon put a stop to our frivolity. Reaching the sea, we turned left into a firing range. Lord protect the illiterate and the short-sighted from Cowden Range. They might miss the dire warnings and the red flags and lights, and get blown to pieces.

All seemed quiet. We entered the range trying to curb our inquisitiveness, keeping strictly to the path and giving a wide berth to odd bits of finned metal. In the distance we saw the last of three black and yellow chequered control boxes, marking the end of no-mans-land. Around its base a crowd gathered, and they were examining our every move through binoculars. We were in for it this time. Cowed, we approached, proffering our wrists for the 'cuffs. 'Have you seen it?' asked several of the multitude. 'Seen what?' 'Why the blue cheeked bee-eater of course'. 'Well, er, no. How do you do. Have you come far?'

A most distinctive species in its own right, the wax-jacketed twitcher had come to Great Cowden from all over England. It came en-masse, to see a bird, packing the normally deserted country lane like a horde on Cup Final Day. Escaping the forest of necks we scrambled to the sands for the hike to Mappleton.

Bags permanently packed, the residents of Cowden Cliff sleep in scuba gear, knowing that come the great storm, wetting the bed would take on a whole new meaning. Defying the edge, the cabins are strung out, doomed outposts of Mappleton whose own battle against erosion is to receive timely aid. A £1.7 million coastal defence scheme, consisting of a rock wall and ancillary timber groynes, is to begin shortly, hopefully ending centuries of decline. Having time to spare we went to see if the money will be well spent.

Home to 100 souls, Mappleton is succoured by the mother church of All Saint's, and by several old inns wherein displayed are memorial photographs of long since vanished buildings. The constant plight of the surviving village is illustrated by the Church Registers:-

> "Distance from church to the sea cliff in a direct line:-
> April 20th 1786 . . . . 28 chains 76 links
> April 17th 1858 . . . . 21 chains 62 links."

For readers under 90 years of age who will be familiar with more modern measuration, I will elucidate: there was a total land loss in 72 years of over 157 yards (143metres) — an average of over 2 yards (1.8 metres) per year.

We spent some time poking around the church which was restored in 1855 using stone from a wrecked ship. I wondered? Would many eyes notice the building's strange absence of gutters, or the quirky nature of its old tracker-actioned single manual organ? My back packed Oracle noticed all, proving the bellows by giving theivories a quick tickle, whilst I examined the monument to the Brough family, and several windows replaced following damage by an air raid in 1941. We left, annotating the architectural omissions in our Pevsner's as we paced out the remaining 10 or so chains to the beach.

Heading towards Hornsea, I took a bearing on Rolston Hall, the one time home of Marshall of the Admiralty William Brough, whose family monument we had seen in Mappleton church. Brough's enemy, the American buccaneer John Paul Jones (more of his skullduggery later), had similar notions, loosing off his cannon whenever he sailed within range of the target chimneys. Keeping one's head down is obviously not just a recent preoccupation in these parts.

Hornsea

Bridlington

Flamborough

Verdancy is the word. It springs to mind at the sight of trees, ranks of trees, chestnut, oak and doctored elm, an emerald swathe relieving the drought of the barren miles. Graced by trees, acres of parkland, golden beaches and an incomparable mere, the largest freshwater lake in Yorkshire, Hornsea is a prescription for old fashioned frolics — fresh air, sand and liberal doses of brine; splashed, poured and squirted. Carting regulation buckets, inflatable dinghys and newly purchased water pistols, having met our troupes, we clattered into a boarding-house near the promenade. Typically it began to rain. Undeterred, stout-lipped, determined to enjoy our sojourn even in monsoon, we sallied forth into the roke, waterproofed to the nines, squinting through the swirl incognito.

The award winning folk museum on Newbegin was an interesting shelter from the rain. Bulging with exhibits, and a curious wax model of Rose Carr, a Victorian lady renowned for her prodigious strength, the museum can while away an inclement hour. Yet Albion's sun dallies for no man. A chink in the clouds and we emerged to find Bettison's Tower, an edifice gloryfying in hot food. This folly of 1844 was built at the end of Willows Drive by Hull businessman, W. Bettison. The contrivance enabled staff to see their punctilious master's carriage from afar, allowing them to serve his hot dinner immediately he crossed the threshold. The leg weary drudges were salad devotees.

At the end of Newbegin, near Market Place, stands the 13th century parish church dedicated to St. Nicholas, the patron saint of sailors. Tugged by impatient mini-mariners, we never saw the place and our estrangement-from the keyboard continued. We were shanghaied to the mere.

A remnant glacial lake, Hornsea Mere has been an important fishery and recreational asset since medieval times. Coveted by the contesting abbots of Meaux and York, it witnessed a day-long duel of champions in 1260. Apart from the war years, when it was boomed to prevent landings by sea-planes, little has ruffled its serenity. Near the quieter western fringes, perch, tench, roach and specimen pike prowl the depths, and rare waterfowl preen unmolested, whilst off the eastern boathouse jolly-rogered cads cruise with wet intent.

Twenty minutes afloat and my baling arms were numb. I pulled for the bank, opting for the comparative safety of the beach and my inevitable pit. The burial party dragooned me down Eastgate, passing the old cobbled White Cottage where 'Lawrence of Arabia' was once entertained. In our fealty to sand we had a lot in common.

Splat! The orificial calling card broke my tropical dream. I peered out of the bespattered window and dressed leaving my family abed. It was raining again.

Coward's 'Mad Dogs and Englishmen' is a refrain for all seasons. There they were, as we set out, on the Floral Hall Bowling Green, demented Tykes, riveted to their near buoyant jack. 'Walking! In this lot! You must be crackers', joked one of the knot. Heads down into the squall we laughed, and struck out for Skipsea.

Butting the wind we saw nothing of inland Atwick with its famous cross and village green. Cold and bedraggled and in no mood for detours, we pushed on, anxious to reach Bridlington by nightfall.

After the umpteenth leisure park at Skirlington, we came to the vacant site of Cleeton village. As lost as

Atlantis, not a vestige of 'Clay-Town' remains. Yet, occupation of the cliffs near Skipsea continues in the form of flooboard palaces, cobbled together from anything that wioll deflect a drop of rain. Amazed at the power of the nail, we passed the line of hill-billy shacks, some awaiting a demolishing wind, others gale tight and freshly painted with hollyhocks at the door. 'Who says we can't afford digs this year Grandma? We'll make our own. There's that old garden shed, and we've no use for t'kennel since Rover died'. I admire the builders of those ramshackle homes. No credit card holidays for them. Roll out the Union Jack for their castles of economy and improvisation. Heath Robinson would be proud.

Our visits to Skipsea village, its church and ancient motte and bailey castle, like that to Atwick, would await more leisured days. Bee-line tramping has its limitations.

We crossed the Barmston Drain. Magically the clouds melted, the sun doffed his Panama and suddenly time could wait. We felt like exploring.

On the beachward side, Barmston has terminal blight, amoebic mobile homes marring the scimitar curve of Bridlington Bay. The contagion ends abruptly a stride inland, the tiny church of All Saint's and the Jacobean manor house of the Boyntons, reminders of a village that was once the military capital of East Yorkshire.

We rested by a vestigial pond, watching a coot and talking to a greybeard, a 'gravel catcher's' son who had witnessed great change, transforming Barmston from a remote rural community to a pleasure ground for tourists. The man showed us his wooden house near the fine old hospital of 1726. Built of Scandinavian timber, the home has withstood the ravages of nature for nigh on a hundred years. Barmston's honour guard of elms has proved less resilient, succumbing to Dutch elm disease, those lifeless trunks cut and stripped, hoisted on a local hillock as sinister monuments, a crown of gnarled entreating thorns thrusting to the sky stone-dead.

A momentary lull in the bombardment of the English summer and English flesh is denuded, bulge naked, bumps, folds, flaps and pendulous extremities exposed for an orgy of mass, masochistic peeling. The instinctive unrobing is triggered by the merest beam, and so withinminutes the sands at Barmston were the scene of a stampede of scantily clad women and children, the Klondyke charge brought up at the rear by a straggle of husbands, lumbered with deckchairs, windbreaks and enough provisions to feed an army. Galvanised into heliolotry, with brave abandon, we too removed apparel. Slinging our boots we toe-poked the brine.

Splashing northward we came to Fraisthorpe beach, a traverse of which was unavoidable. Unexploded shells we could cope with. The debauching perils of Fraisthorpe were a different kettle of walruses. Men of decorum, we fixed our eyes front, strenuously avoiding the assemblage of blubber. Then we spied her, a confronting vista of a woman monopolising the surf, a bulimious sow, slurping a pot of whelks and displacing more water than the Ark Royal. We were put off naturism for life.

We entered Bridlington looking for Hilderthorpe Road. I found the address of our unsuspecting host in an old college diary. 'Pimples' McLean had invited me to call 'one day'. After fifteen years that day had arrived.

The following day, pulling on our waterproofs we were consoled. It had been the wettest June on record. Bridlington was awash.

Second only to Scarborough as Yorkshire's premier tourist resort, Bridlington heaved with its seasonal throng, braced and belted, inured, resigned, drip-dried seekers of that great British dream — the seaside holiday, to be enjoyed come hell or high water. Families flitted from mean cafés to amusement arcades. I grieved for the parents whose precious fortnight ebbed, and I grieved for their children. Denied the simple pleasure of Bridlington's excellent beaches, they were ensnared by those dens of vacuous diversion. Shelter seeking moths to an

*SKIPSEA ... cobbled together from anything that would deflect a
drop of rain.*

BRIDLINGTON BAYLE GATE...see the indelible crest of the old priors.

electronic flame, we mingled, clenching our principled coin, conspicuous non-belligerents in the battle of the screens. Repelled, we escaped into the rain.

Fringed with golden sands, Bridlington Bay has, in fair weather, abundant charms. Terrestrials, vigorous and lazy, are amply accommodated on the extensive strand, whilst aquatics find tacking room enough. But when sky and sea swill in grey convocation, only littering gulls brave the waves, and so I found the south-shore yacht compound stoutly locked. I read its cautionary sign and vowed never to commit myself to the deep again. 'No boat may launch unless it has flares and compass, paddles or oars, whistle or lanyard, bailer or bucket, fire extinguisher, anchor, 150′ of rope, life-jackets, and third party insurance of minimum £50,000.'

During the First World War, German U-boats stalked the bay, sinking many ships including *HMS Falmouth* which was torpedoed in only 60 feet of water. Normally a safe anchorage, except in severe northerly gales, the bay can be churned to fatal broth, boiling over the deceptive Smethwick Sands lying east of the town. On 10 February 1871 about 30 ships and 70 seamen together with the gallant lifeboat crew were lost to the Great Gale.

After miles of rural peace, the impact of a large town is disconcerting. Bridlington's streets were choked with traffic. Contrived and artificial, many of its strictly functional buildings preside over yellow-ribboned roads, a creeping scourge of 'pay and display' car parks, and signs, hundreds of signs, rude, insistent, competitive signs, tentacled invitations to 'Pay Here' plastered on every wall. The blackboard humour of an optimistic deck-chair attendant relieved the gloom. 'Outlook bright and sunny. Queue here', instructed his board, carefully protected by an umbrella. 'Looks like I'm in for a quiet day', said the man venturing a meteorological hand into the rain. 'I've got to stay open even when it pours. Good job I'm not on commission.'

Breathing a cocktail of fresh fish and diesel oil, we approached the harbour, a modern facility sited at the outfall of the lovely Gypsey Race, a freshwater stream that once marked the terminus of an old bullion routebetween Ireland and the continent. Gilt-edged tourists and fishing provide today's income, 40 trawlers and 17 cobles steaming up to 200 miles offshore in search of cod, haddock, plaice, ling and skate. Landlubbers may inspect the glass-eyed bounty from a purpose built viewing platform above the harbour wall. Those with sea-legs can join the ever increasing convoys of amateur fishermen who fish the wrecks. For the casual angler, there hangs a salutary tale.

Promised bulging freezers, my friend and I arrived in Bridlington one cold November morn, having booked our maiden voyage aboard the good boat *Yorkshire Lass*. We were the oddest of peas in a pitching pod. Oil-skinned and sea-booted, our shipmates stared, shaking their salt pickled heads at our Sunday-best attire. The captain grinned as the first volley of spray soaked us through.

The next six entrail spewing hours were the most wretched of our lives. Bilious rats, we cowered in the bilges, slithering in a morass of sea-water, vomit and the innards of freshly gutted cod. Caring not a fig if Moby Dick himself had been hauled aboard, we wallowed on, bezel struck, praying for torment's end.

Our ordeal must not deter visitors from pleasure cruising on more substantial craft. The *Yorkshire Belle*, and the *Flamborian*, offer delightful summer outings to Flamborough Head and the spectacular cliffs beyond. Both boats have bars, private ladies' saloons, music, live running commentary and toilets, so gunwale droopings are avoided.

In the deepening trough not a propeller turned. Pulling our hoods to the wind we set out for the Old Town and its church, passing Bridlington's tropical isle. Splashing in the artificial surf of Leisure World, children cavorted behind the runnelled glass.

Yorkshire has more monastic ruins than any other

county in the Kingdom, evocative, skeletal remains of an incredibly beautiful architectural genre smashed by Henry's hand. Standing in sky-clad naves, imaginations usually need guide book prod, but in the remarkably preserved Bridlington Priory, time-flashed initiates incant the ancient rites, ancestral spontaniety seeping from a hundred gargoyled mouths. We explored in reverential silence.

Founded by the Augustinian order in 1113 AD, the priory grew to be one of the most wealthy and powerful religious establishments in the north, producing a succession of famous priests. Of the thirty-one priors, John-de-Bridlington (1366-1379) is best remembered for his learning and exceptional sanctity, acknowledged in 1401 by canonisation. His grave behind the high altar became a shrine, reputed to be the scene of numerous miracles, attracting many distinguished pilgrims, including Kings Henry IV and Henry V.

Robert the Scribe, the fourth prior, made his mark in writing and in transcribing voluminous works. Peter of Langtoft achieved similar literary success, producing several books, notably a Chronicle of England written in French verse. Perhaps the most interesting canon was Sir George Ripley, a renowned philosopher and alchemist, whose scientific prowess was recognised by the Pope, who relieved him from the strictures of his order so that he could devote himself to science. In 1538 the line was axed. The last prior, William Wode, had been actively involved in the ill-fated Pilgrimage of Grace, and along with many other insurrectionists, he was executed.

After dissolution, Henry's jackals moved in, dismembering the work of four centuries. Ignominiously some stonework from the priory buildings and transepts went to bolster the harbour wall, yet the great nave, set apart as a parish church, went unmolested. Carefully re-erected in the church after years of burial outside are exquisite fragments of the original cloisters. What craftsmanship. Even pagans must have wept at such destruction.

About one hundred yards from the priory stands the Bayle Gate, the last of four fortified entrances, built as a protection against marauding pirates. The structure houses a small museum, owned by the local authority. On the west side of the gate three 'B's' are displayed on an armorial shield, the indelible crest of the old priors, stamping an inalienable ownership that defies the legitimising years. What of the inheritors of such monastic property, those elitist generations whose privilege derives from larcenous spoil? Theirs is surely spurious title, centuries of legal machinations altering thereality not one jot. The church should have the most compelling case in the annals of litigation; so ponder, looking to your criminal antecedents, you pompous upper classes.

Our visit concluded, we left the church, but the organist's rear-end had monopolised his stool, and my chum was peeved. I led him down the Old Town High Street and Westgate, architecturally Bridlington's finest thoroughfares, housing a convent, numerous antique shops, a wonderfully unaltered pharmacy and the Ye Olde Star Inn, purveyor of victuals guaranteed to soothe the grouchy breast.

Restored, we left the soggy town and regained the shore, wondering if Saint Swithen too was peeved. We were soaked to our discoloured skin, trickling dye from bargain Taiwanese tartan shirts blotching sodden trousers that clung like limpets at high tide.

Llamas were never meant to endure such storms. In the zoological enclosure to Sewerby Park they cowered, sad exiles of the pampas. Bought by Bridlington Corporation in 1934, Sewerby has a well stocked children's zoo, and a number of other family attractions — gardens, putting greens, an archery range and a toddlers play area, all set around the 18th century Elizabethan style mansion, housing period treasures and a museum devoted to the great aviator, Amy Johnson. We postponed our visit to the park to a brighter day, skirting its ha-ha, not in jovial mood.

Above Sewerby Rocks the cliffs rise in chalky procession to Flamborough Head, the most prominent geological feature of our eastern seaboard, a thrusting bastion of chalk overlain with boulder clay, rising to giddy heights. A natural fortress on the seaward side, the headland was protected landward during the Iron Age by deep excavations running for some 2½ miles. Axe and arrow heads from this mis-named Danes Dyke provide evidence of occupation by warring tribes who preceded the Norsemen by several centuries. A scheduled ancient monument, the densely wooded earthwork is now a nature trail, its ravines providing the ideal habitat for roe-deer, badgers, rare orchids and a host of resident and migrant birds. Rain muzzled, nothing stirred. We squelched through the arboreal sponge in silence, images of a hot-bath the mirageous spur. Teeth clenched, we bore on, as desolate as Noah, metronomic steps plodding to the sound of a storm-gonged bell that pitched beyond the reef.

For several minutes we stood on the peak above South Landing, voyeurs diverted by the entertainment of two hard pressed divers who tussled to beach a dinghy. Taking a closer look we braved the shingle, still detached until the swell tossed the craft onto an awaiting trailer. Punctured and swamped, it seemed doomed. 'What the hell', I said as our boots bit the surf. 'We're pissing wet through already!' Concerted heaving inched the boat ashore, and within five minutes it was high and dry. Fuelled with thanks we marched for Flamborough village.

Using wifely logic I examined the curtains. They were clean, so I ventured a knock. 'It's a man mam', yelled the jam-smeared receptionist. 'Bed and breakfast? Surely', said the landlady wiping her hands on a pinafore dusted with flour. 'Come in'. Mired, yet house-trained, we bridled at the mat. 'Don't want to mucky your lovely white carpet love', said my chum. 'Oh you needn't bother mister, follow me'. A sentinel of the staircase, the aspidistra had stood on its landing perch since Dick's days. Decades of immobility were fading fast. A wayward sleeve and it was condemned to disintegration, tread and riser conspiring a bouncy annihilation. It lay at the end of a trail of freshly watered soil — a sundered wreck. Woe befell us. The landlady had been rolling pastry. The baton of admonishment was close at hand.

We awoke the following morning with throbbing heads. Not from actual blows from that terrible club —brandishment had been enough to scare us stiff — no, after clearing up the mess and grovelling, we had high-tailed it to the 'Royal Dog and Duck' for a surfeit of ale, insistently supplied by two grateful divers.

On pearly mornings like that I can cope with a headache. Levitating sunbeams prised us from our beds, and, in still damp clothes we stowed our treasure chest and tip-toed into the dawn. We had smugglers' business at Flamborough's North Landing.

Swirled by storms and treacherous currents, the forbidding Flamborough cliffs claimed an average of 5 vessels per year until the lighthouse was built in 1806. Flamborough light, its pulse extending for up to 21 miles, and an ear-splitting Fog Station, warn of the continuing perils.

The coast hereabouts is riven and writhed, tormented by the eternal rush and thrash, sculpted into spectacular forms — arches, caves, stacks, thunderous blow-holes, and steep coves where the Flamborian risks his keel. North Landing is merely that, a place, when the weather allows, for the opportunist fisherman to winch himself dry. With only dive-bombing gulls as raucous witness, we plunged into this romantic den, sliding through rock pools to a pink-tinged cavern, a marbled hall of Triton, cold and gurgling, the deflected shafts shimmering on the roof of Robin Lythe's Cave. Like that famous smuggler immortalised by R.D. Blackmore in his novel 'Mary Anerley', we secreted our chest and fled the tide. Some weeks later, guided by his treasure map, Tom discovered the prize. The stories he told his friends were worth a king's ransom.

SEWERBY HALL ... home of the Amy Johnson museum.

NORTH LANDING ... a romantic den.

SPURN LIFEBOAT STATION ... an insubstantial shed.

BARMSTON ... old hospital of 1726.

SEWERBY CLIFFS
... a fine hike to Bridlington.

After enjoying a girding breakfast (we had presented a replacement plant to our host) we went birdwatching.

The cliffs between North Landing and Selwicks Bay have been eroded into inaccessible coves, providing nesting acommodation for thousands of squabbling puffins, razorbills, guillemots, shags, fulmars and kittiwakes, soaring and diving in cantankerous flight, contesting every fin and crevice. Observation is not for the nauseous, nor for we comrades of the fatty pan. I shunned the precipice and the shivering sight of my chum, hanging with photographic intent.

There is a picnic table above this bay, embowered with rank weeds masking the gougings of an old gun emplacement. Hewn from the rudest of planks, it is crumbed and paper-cupped but candelabra could not grace the grain more. Billow sparked, attended by Adam, a venerable sea-stack, this is the finest sandwich bar in England, a breath-taking belvedere, a transmuter of bread and cheese. Savouring our gourmet crusts, we gazed spellbound.

Near the bay stand a snowy white lighthouse and a toposcope commemorating a famous naval battle fought off the headland in September 1779. The founder of the American Navy, the impudent buccaneer John Paul Jones, attacked a convoy of Baltic merchantmen with a heavily armed squadron of 4 ships — the *Bonhomme Richard*, *Alliance*, *Pallas* and *Vengeance*. Two English men-of-war, the *Seraphis* and the *Countess of Scarborough* intervened, and in eerie moonlight cannons flamed for over two hours. Outmatched, the *Countess of Scarborough* yielded to the *Pallas*, but *Seraphis* fought on, inflicting terrible damage to the enemy flagship. After hand-to-hand fighting the *Seraphis* was overcome and eventually commandered by Jones, who transferred his flag from the foundering *Bonhomme Richard*, finally limping some two weeks later into the Dutch port of Texel.

The defence of the realm has come on a pace since those broadside days. A fire-plummed Tornado sped by, reaching Middlesbrough in minutes. We would take weeks yet. The distraction of earning a living interrupted our tour. We sulked back to our city holes displeased.

Flamborough

Filey

Scarborough

After days of cogitation I finally came up with a ruse for absconding from work. I sat a wax dummy at my desk and arranged with a friend to fill up my waste-paper basket every night. But for the fire-bell, I would not have been missed.

De-mob happy, I binged on a transport café breakfast before setting out for Thornwick Bay, where I had once endured an appalling seven day holiday with a pimply friend. Puberal stirrings had caused us to shun family outings and go caravanning in search of girls. We got gulls and 168 hours of rain. Supping Tizer with only occasional sprints to the john or camp shop to break the monotony, we whiled away the hours, studying copies of 'Health and Efficiency' and 'Lady Chatterley's Lover'. Sometimes we played cards, semi-naked, shivering under yards of damp clothing, existing on beans and sausage sandwiches, reaching, between deals, for our bean-tin balers as the ceiling leaked- I examine the photographic evidence of our pluvial servitude, and see, almost breaking into a smile, the numb creatures in the 'Columbo' style gaberdine macs. In the days before television, a man in a nearby coastguard station promised us a peep at his radar screen if we promised to be good boys. The thrill of the week.

Decades on from that holiday my thrilling days are over, and I am now more appreciative of good old Thornwick which is unsullied and little changed. Youthful pre-occupations precluded a visit to Bempton Cliffs all those years ago, but see my enthusiasm now. Roll up! Roll up! Before your dizzy eyes an avian

spectacular! See the giddy cliff, the blur of feather and the kindergarten of chicks, bill to bill, clamouring for their fish stew. One of the greatest shows on earth is yours for free, the flighty stars being wonderfully protected by the RSPB, who have built a number of vantage points and an informative visitor centre in the fields close by.

Dripping early morning dew, I took up my bird-watching station at Bempton squinting through fog at phantoms curving a wondrous sea-arched rainbow that quivered in the haze. Until comparatively recently, this site, the only one in mainland Britain to support gannets, was threatened by commercial egg collectors or 'climmers'. Tethered by a rope belayed to an iron stake driven into the cliff top, 'climmers' were lowered down the chalk walls, gathering up to 400 eggs per day in linen bags slung either side of their shoulders. Sold to collectors and for food and patent leather processing, the eggs continued to be harvested until 1954 when the trade became illegal. Today there can, in season, be in excess of 70,000 breeding pairs of birds in the area at any one time. That gives me an idea for my garden. I could borrow a 'climmers' kit and never have to buy 'Growmore' again.

By the time I dragged myself away from my perch a sizeable group of bird-watchers had arrived, sporting state-of-the-art binoculars that put my toy-town tubes to shame. That's another item for Santa's list.

The great sweep of Filey Bay spurred me along through the scrubby Speeton Hills to Reighton and Hunmanby, and the gaunt skeleton of the former Butlins Holiday Camp, whose demise contrasts sharply with the fortunes of the adjacent Primrose Valley. In many ways, I prefer the shacks of Skipsea to the ultra modern caravans I found at Primrose Valley. Gregarious lemmings sign there for wall to wall carpet, laser operated toilets and 5 years of repayment misery. The once green acres are blotted out with caravans and with caravanners, like migrating Wildebeest cramming into camp shops, arcades, pubs and pleasure grounds, leaving not an untrampled blade of grass for miles. I hoped Filey

BRIDLINGTON ... I'll have the yellow one.

NORTH LANDING ... cathedral cave.

town had fared better.

Seminal Filey, unspoilt and uncrowded, the inspiration for my love of leg room. During the 1950's I bowled many a leg-spinner on those capacious sands.

Filey was the base for a succession of joyous family holidays, enthralling from the moment we left Leeds City Station with our suitcases bulging with clothes and diverse foodstuffs, each child being allotted a quota of ham, corned beef, sardines, cling peaches, tea and evaporated milk by the case. Wrapped in steam, fixing Lilliputian stares at the towering men of the footplate, tamers of romantically named engines like *Braes of Derwent* and *The Badsworth*, what child could remain po-faced? What coble emigrés would not wonder at the sumptuous carriages empanelled in tropical woods and decorated with pictures of far off isles? After the dourness of the town, these journeys were magical. From grime to chlorophylled flush in a puff of smoke. In Filey we were met by barrow lads, who for a shilling, would trundle our luggage to Collins Camp and the shack 'Sunbeam', deficient in running water and sanitary facilities but only a full toss from the sands. Stomping the crease once more I sighed in sweet nostalgia.

Memories are soured by modernity. Having met my family, I booked into a likely looking boarding house. My opinions of Filey suddenly nose-dived.

The effect on my nose was very pertinent. To put it in plain Yorkshire parlance, the place was foisty; black-bright; mucky to its cob-webbed roof, the domain of a fag-drooped crone whose face had seen more embalming than Nefertiti's. The bed linen was a disgrace, and the tide marked bath! It would not have passed muster in a farm yard. Making a pointed excuse about our low resistance to bubonic plague, we left, with young Tom in tears.

I was vexed with Filey and Tom was wailing for his promised weekend. Where would we go? 'South', I said, remembering a farmhouse I had passed near Flam-borough. For the first time in my journey I went withershins, retracing my steps...by car! My nib shatters at the word.

The occasional smack of a yardstick is a salutary thing. To appreciate the good in life we need to plummet thebad. Chastened, we examined the 'B/B' sign and entered the drive. Optimism returned. Even the drinking trough looked clean. Dodging a tonguey welcome, we paddled over a threshold scattered with wellies. Enter a proper landlady, scrubbed-armed and pinnied, the matriarch of a rose-clad palace which was as clean as a fresh sucked teat. The helter-skelter banister, burnished by generations of rustic bums, led to our room, homely and welcoming, stuffed with venerable furniture that reeked of wax polish. It was a rambling house. It needed to be. There were thirteen toothbrushes in the pot.

Returning to Filey we played cricket on the sands below the Coble Landing, where Yorkshire's famous fishing boats are hauled to dry. A sturdy clinker-built craft whose design can be traced back to the Viking longship, the coble is ideal for its principal purpose of crabbing, long-lining and salmon netting. Stumps drawn, we ran to welcome a home coming boat as she was dragged ashore by a tractor. Up the ramp she came, sliding on her keel, nudging the brightly painted sister prows outside Jimmy Corrigan's amusement arcade — a strange and raucous bedfellow. Blinking in the sunlight, inquisitive troglodytes took time out from feeding coin to goggle. Scoffing at the catch they returned to their slots. As for me, pooh-poohing grey hairs, I said goodbye to the gang, donned training shoes and leapt from the blocks. Enervating Filey has that effect on you, setting even Chelsea pensioners to the trot.

Girded by a five mile swathe of beach, the bay is Filey's glory, the backdrop for breathless fun and loafing. After a healthy gallop on the sands, an exhausting sailing expedition, or a hike through Crescent Gardens, the town is a great place for relaxing. Some complain of ossification, and to be frank, Filey has its

*FILEY BRIGG ... constructed by the Devil in a half-hearted
attempt at bridging the North Sea.*

FILEY ... a problem for Santa?

FILEY ... silver strands.

SCARBOROUGH – THE GRAND HOTEL ... an upturned sow.

SCARBOROUGH ... museum close.

47

share of retirement homes and a sparsity of nightlife and the type of organised entertainment that appeals to the younger masses. Visitors may indeed nod off, but it is likely to be as a result of sheer exhaustion rather than the sag of old bones.

Panting, I aired my toes in the churchyard of St. Oswald's, contemplating the foot-sore deeds of one time incumbent, Arthur Neville Cooper, a hero to all walking men. Canon Cooper came to Filey in 1879 and began a series of international walking tours that were prodigious, visiting Italy, Ireland, Iceland, Denmark, Belgium and Portugal on 10 shillings a day expenses. A fun-loving man, nonchalant of distance, bad weather and blisters (his remedy was to pour two pennyworth of whisky into the offending shoes), the canon recorded his adventures in a series of inspirational books. 'With Knapsack and Notebook', 'Tales of My Tramps' and 'Quaint Talks About Long Walks' are fine examples. An eager convert to the Yorkshire creed of 'eating all, supping all, and paying now't' — a man after my own wallet — he is commemorated by a simple gravestone and a chancel plaque in the church he served so well for 55 years. Greasing my feet for the next leg of my marathon along the Cleveland Way, like Cooper I warmed to the prospect of 'that never absent relish that toil imparts'. Swinging my sack I headed for Filey Brigg.

Projecting for nearly a mile below the ramparts of Carr Nase Cliffs, the spectacular Filey Brigg compels exploration. Bent on annihilation, the sea hurls against the Brigg in foul weather. At low water the reef is seemingly placid and inviting, scooped with rock pools, strewn with great boulders, perfidious magnets drenched by occassional rogue waves that probe for the unwary. Tradition asserts that the Brigg was constructed by the Devil in a half-hearted attempt at bridging the North Sea, a humourous notion dispelled by the chill of a warning tablet let into the rocks by the Page family who grieve for a lost relative.

Guided by tide tables, respectfully I set off in search of fossils, heartily cheered by the sight of my chum, scurrying down Ravine Road to make our rendezvous. He too had broken the sedentary yoke and was elated, feeling like a new-born babe, wriggling and giggling, back-slapping, relishing the prospect of a few days away from his desk.

We pocketed a mound of specimens and in drizzleslithered up the greasy cliff on permanent ropes provided for the benefit of anglers. We were cast down. Without warning, a thundering Tornado shaved the peak, almost singeing our hair with its after-burner. We held on shouting abuse at the long gone pilot.

Panting, we made the top and viewed the glorious Brigg as she braved a stiff north-easter, cheering at the cylinders of aquamarine coiling for massed assault. Unleashed, the bores crashed down with terrific force, shooting up frenzied columns of water as though a battery of shells had been detonated in quick turn, trapped air booming in clouds of spray, and the ledges cascading with creamy foam. On the leeward side, the sea was comparatively calm. Was this the Roman's 'well-havened bay' that Ptolemy refers to? Certainly some traces of an artificial pier jutting out at right angles to the Brigg have been found. The reef would provide the ideal site for a harbour, and proposals were once drawn up by the House of Commons for the construction of a facility large enough to accommodate the entire British fleet, although the plans came to nothing.

The headland upon which we stood was the site of a Roman signal station, and the subject of a 1944 planning enquiry to consider a housing scheme proposed for 320 acres of Church Farm. Thankfully the enquirers decided against development so near the sea, recognising the unique heritage of this wild and desolate place.

We saw our destination sunning itself whilst we soaked, the distinctive silhouette of Scarborough Castle marking the first pause on the 93 mile long Cleveland Way, the most varied long distance footpath in Britain, beginning in Filey and running north-west along the coast to Saltburn, and thence southward skirting the North York Moors to Helmsley. Already clarted up to the eyeballs, courtesy of the RAF, we slid on the first mile of the well worn track, lamenting the state of well worn soles.

The path crests the sheer North and Newbiggin Cliffs, which resemble weathered slag heaps and host vast roosts of stockdoves. A precipitous drop onto the otherwise inaccessible beach at Brewster Hole invites the adventurous to chance a low-tide hike to the Brigg. Several people have paid for this folly with their lives. The warning of a faded, hardly legible sign is lost on impatient and reckless fools.

At the foot of Grisethorpe Cliffs, extensive rocky scars ribbon the shore, capped at the northern end by the calcareous grit of Red Cliff Point. In this vicinity an ancient oaken coffin was unearthed from a large tumulus in 1834. I was to make the acquaintance of the skeletal occupant of the box later in the day in Scarborough's Rotunda Museum.

The season had guillotined the tourists' year. They had surrendered their marshalled sepulchres atop Lebberston Cliff en-masse. All was stowed, wrapped and bagged. Axles were chained, sightless windows boarded up with cheap hardboard, the cherished inches entombed in blackness until Spring. Past dormant gardens we hurried in a heavy shower, seeking the shelter of a pill box overlooking Cayton Bay. From the gunslits, I scanned a beach once coveted by the German High Command. Their operation 'Sealion' was scuppered following the Battle of Britain in 1940, and the beach remains unmarked except for two disfiguring fortifications dislodged from the cliff by erosion.

Seasonal landward invasions of the beach are mounted from the nearby Wallis's tourist complex, more sophisticated than most, offering a full range of leisure facilities and modern family chalets, a distinctive breed of accommodation immensely superior to the 'Hi-de-Hi' kennels I remember so well from the 1950's. Having dodged the rain, we aimed for the northern arm of the bay which is clothed to the water's edge in a maquis type of woodland — a chiney den of holly and dense blackthorn recurring in pockets all along the northern march. Veering off into the dark and oozy dell of Knipe Point, a nature reserve owned by the National Trust, we descended to 'Johnny Flinton's Harbour', a quiet natural cove, hard by the perilous rocks that lead on to CornelianBay, named after the semi-precious stones that are supposed to be there for the plucking. Ever keen to fund a night of jollity, we scoured in vain, until inundated boots told us it was time to leave for Scarborough.

The scene of mis-spent youth (I played snooker as well) Scarborough brings back fond memories. From the earliest days I remember the angelic landlady of our perennial 'digs' in Northstead Manor Gardens. She brought an unsullied lad his nightly Ovaltine. And I recall the wonderful times with Mum and Dad — the impromptu boxing lessons on the beach — picnics, grandstand views of the re-enactment of the Battle of the River Platte by model warships on Peasholm Park lake, visits to Gala Land, and rattling jaunts by narrow gauge railway to Scalby Mills. The glimmerings are painful now. The old folks have gone, yet the legacy beams on in young Tom.

In coxcombed adolescence I returned to Scarborough with several friends. We stayed at a fashionable hotel, drank copious amounts of ale, emboldened, pursued the odd girl, (odd indeed — matinal inspection proved we chose them by weight!) and indulged in pranks. The black-faced soap was fairly innocuous, and the 'Dirty Fido' simulation on the dining room table was harmless enough. It was the two-bob box of powdered horse hair, described on the lid as being 'worse than a cart-load of fleas' that was really evil. Pyjama sprinkled, the full dose was deployed at the strategic orifice, inducing a paroxysm of scratching. Convinced he had contracted some vile disease, the frantic victim stood in the sink dousing himself with water. My amusement turned to remorse at the sight of pain. I have never used itching powder since.

Photographs of our beds sparkled in full colour. 'Inspection invited' said the caption underneath. 'That'll do for me. This strap could cut cheese' barked my tired chum, dropping his camera bag.

From our room among the chimney pots we looked out at the panorama of roofs and the unmistakable trade mark of Scarborough — the 12th century castle built on a 250 feet headland between two bays. Then the heating system gurgled, heralding our arrival. We stripped and wallowed and de-grimed, and regilded rejoined the streets in civvy shoes. The sensation of wearing boots lingered for hours.

Audible tums spurred the quest for fish and chips. A snaking queue led us to our goal, a dingy back-street dispenser of fist full crispness and flavour. In Tyke fashion we ordered 'twice' (each) and wuffed the lot.

Thirst thrust, we next sought out the old dives, those tap-room snugs where we had quaffed our under-age gills of Rose's Bitter. Swamped in an antipodean tide, such traditional English pubs are becoming a rarity, so hurrah for The Hole-in-the-Wall, a shrine to aboriginal brews, a fount of revival ales with resounding names like Old Ma Pardoe's, Pendle Witches Brew, Titanic Premium and Old Peculiar. Evaluation of the hand-pulled wares was a long and pleasurable toil. We sipped, half glass by half glass, until my normally staid and reticent co-sampler threw propriety to the wind. He ordered pints and even winked at the bar-maid. Suffice to say, we simply rolled home. I led the tip-toe climb up the stairs as behind me a hitherto repressed childhood ambition took wing. For whom the breakfast gong tolled? It tolled for me. The following morning the sour-faced puss was not amused. A light sleeper, she deliberately burnt my eggs, whilst the perpetrator slumbered on. I heard his confessional and put my fossils in his bag.

Adjusting my straps on The Esplanade, I puffed out my chest at the twinkling expanse of South Bay, recognising a scene that constantly brightens my city room. 'Scarborough Lights' by Atkinson Grimshaw —the famous Victorian master of chiaroscuro from my home town of Leeds — is a beguiling canvas, depicting a light pricked bay hushed in romantic veils of moonlight — a hallmark feature of the artist's work. Grimshaw was a Scarborough resident between 1876 and 1879, living at the eccentric castellated 'Castle-by-the-Sea' on Mulgrave Place. Four typical examples of his pointillist style of painting, including the dramatic 'Burning of the Spa Saloon' may be seen in the Crescent Art Gallery.

A tour-de-force by another local giant, architect Cuthbert Broderick, whose other major achievements include the Town Hall and Corn Exchange in Leeds, is to be seen across the Spa Bridge. Once the most luxurious hotel in Europe, the Grand, built in 1865, is like an upturned sow, a mammalian edifice offering its pappy extremities to the sky. With its 4 turrets, 365 rooms, 52 chimneys and 12 floors, Broderick foreshadowed the modern addiction to themed attractions by well over a century.

Below the Grand in Vernon Road is the Rotunda Museum built in 1829 to a design by William Smith the 'Father of English Geology'. The museum houses my friend from Grisethorpe Cliffs, and a wealth of archaeological finds from the sites of the Iron Age settlement and Roman signal station on Castle Hill, as well as interesting exhibits charting the history of Scarborough's fishing industry. These include an array of fishermen's good luck charms, stones and magic bones and the dried eyeball of a codfish. A crowning frieze at the top of the building illustrates the entire geology of the Yorkshire coast. My Vibram treads have sampled every layer.

A large and expanding tourist metropolis, traditional, yet adaptive to modern visitor needs, Scarborough can occupy dedicated explorers, dilettantes or shameless idle burghers for weeks. Apart from the timeless diversions of

SCARBOROUGH – SOUTH BAY --- footy and sweep.

the North and South Bays, there are excellent parks and gardens, lavish amusement and water parks, a mere, golf courses, a county cricket ground, theatres, the notorious motorbike circuit of Olivers Mount, and a town-trail taking in such points of interest as Trinity House, The Butter Cross, The Three Mariners Inn, The Spa and Wood End Museum. Had we time, and the shekels, we could have wandered with the best, albeit as bumpkins accoutered for the clart. Even after a bath, polished and city slickered, pavements admit the incongruity, so we were happy to leave the streets, but not before we had paid our respects to Emily Brontë who lies in the churchyard of St. Mary's near the castle. Craggy symbols of church and state, both buildings were damaged by their opposing garrisons during the Civil War. The castle was further bombarded in 1914 by the might of the 'Mailed Fist', two German battleships firing salvo after salvo into the town for fifteen minutes. With 19 people dead, 99 wounded and many buildings damaged or destroyed the nation was rightly indignant. The inhabitants of Scarborough, as contemporary accounts record, displayed the usual Yorkshire phlegm:

"During the Communion Service at St. Martin's, the church was struck by three shells, but the Archdeacon went on with the service, quietly remarking that they were as safe there as anywhere else".

"An old woman whose home was pierced by a shell said 'yes it's a pity, but I wouldn't have minded so much if I hadn't been doing my bit of cleaning'."

"A working man rushing home to see that his wife and children were safe was met at the door by his little girl who cried out joyfully to her mother, 'It's all right now, mother, here's father'."

Scarborough
Robin Hood's Bay
Whitby

In my younger days, Scalby Mills was an outpost. Today it is an appendage of Scarborough, disturbed out of tranquil recognition by a festoonery of cable cars, a miniature railway and Yorkshire Water's piling operations. Their £19 million sewage scheme promises to partly address Scarborough's deplorable complacency on maritime pollution. I get hot under the collar about the need for such schemes. The UK record on environmental abuse is disgraceful. The discarding of unwanted litter by thoughtless individuals is one thing, but the disposing of untreated sewage, chemical and nuclear waste, and the dumping of the mass excreta of that ever insatiable ogre Consumer, all under the blind eye of government, is a scandal threatening our existence. The omnipotent motivation is profitability. If there is a fast buck to be made, exploit it, rape it, pick the bones clean. The only consequence is the consequence of the balance sheet. Short term expediency, long term catastrophe. We hear government ministers pontificating about our future energy needs. Increased output, so they say, can only be achieved by multiplying our nuclear generating capabilities. As recent years have shown, we are all imperilled players in the international game of Russian roulette. So until we have learned to utilise renewable non-polluting energy sources why raise the stakes? Conserve; economise; use less. Pull out the plug. Sit in the dark. Use candles. It could be far more romantic.

Phew! Now that I have got that off my chest (my pal walked ahead, having heard the tirade before) I was set to tackle the stretch of Yorkshire coastline least affected by human intrusion, a 20 mile span of thicketed bays and ravines contrived for wearying the backpacked soul and for spraining ankles. I was glad of a companion.

From Scalby Mills the path climbs to an isthmus between the sea and Scalby Beck, an outfall of the river Derwent still graced by trout, and, according to the enlightened angling club at Hackness, by otters. There may be hope for our species still.

You can quickly turn your back on Scarborough's urban sprawl, but the imprint of its headland fortress draws out the dogged miles. We strode on to Cromer Point, hinterland vistas opening up all the while. Approaching Crook Ness and the road from Burniston village, I felt peckish. The gastric bells were ringing loud, but like a novice I had omitted to pack our food. Salvation was at hand. I had always fancied myself as a frontiersman, a Daniel Boone, a Crusoe sort, making do, improvising, adapting, turning Nature's bounty into food and shelter. As a lad I had worn a Davy Crockett hat (the tail was stealthily scissored from grandma's best stole) and I had made dens and cooked Spam over a fire fuelled with pieces of oil-cloth whose combustion was more suitable for sending messages Indian style than cooking. Now was my chance to excel. Hurrying past the desolate coastguard station at Long Nab with my panting chum in tow, I approached Cloughton Wyke and visions of lunch.

'More haste less speed' (or words to that effect) said my breathless pal as I went 'arse over tit' down the makeshift ladder to the beach.

Cushioned by my load I landed, a terrapin contemplating an unaccustomed sky. I found I had stumbled into a boulder strewn cove fringed by kelp and mossy ledges. All was quiet, save for the squeak of inquisitive wrens and the chafe of the sea.

'Cut the cackle and follow me', I said leading the search for driftwood. 'There! That should make a fine blaze. All we need now is a mackerel. I'm starving'.

On the slab or in the pan, the irridescent mackerel is demeaned only by its abundance. Matching the noble salmon for flavour, this fish is an angler's dream, a lusty fighter, reckless of hook, baited or even bare. I assembled my telescopic rod and battered fixed spool reel and tied on the business end, a home made bijou lure fashioned from a biscuit tin, a rusty treble and a twist of wool. The match was struck and I flung my offering into the waves. And there they were, two beauties, skewered and toasted. Charred fish never tasted so good. I finished off with a palmful of blackberries. 'I could reduce the wife's housekeeping no end', said my pal sucking on a contemplative bone.

We left the embers to the tide and climbed to Roger Trod, where two tractors ploughed within feet of the cliff expunging the path.

'One of the prettiest spots on the entire coast', said I describing the unfolding vista of Hayburn Wyke. 'Woodland, wild flowers and a smashing waterfall'. My chum rummaged for his wide-angled lens. 'There', I said pointing from the heights. 'Tumbling over the gritstone blocks to the beach'.

'That! Why, it's hardly a trickle!'

'What do you want Niagara?'

Compared to Canada's finest, a favourite with honeymooners the world over, Hayburn's fall is a dribble. But it waters a romantic dell to stir the most hesitant heart. Perchance we stumbled on a trysting place, averting eyes and fleeing. Hesitancy had been engulfed. The passionate combatants quivered like fiddlers' elbows.

Erotic suitabilities apart, Hayburn Wyke is chiefly regarded as a picnic spot, a valley of twin streams studded with native hardwoods and rare flowers — golden saxifrage, sanicle, herb robert and grass of parnassus. Even rarer are its fossiliferous liverworts, ferns and cycads. In Victorian days, special excursions ran from York and Scarborough, bringing visitors to explore, for a penny-piece, the specially constructed pathways and grottoes. The classical adaptations did little to disturb the rampancy. Protected by the National Trust it tangles on, checked only by the salt pinching winds contorting the boughs at the seaward fringe.

A quagmire impeded our upward haul. Stoic pack-mules we laboured in silence. Tiredness stills the tongue. It concentrates the limbs. Skirting Staintondale we plodded on deep in thought, passing the thorny wilderness of Beast Cliff.

Dramatic Ravenscar has a taint of melancholia. Its history chills the gaze. On the magnificent 600 feet headland the Vikings raised their fiercesome raven standard. The Romans followed with a signal station, and then came the demented George III, a reluctant guest of Dr. R.C. Hall, a royal physician who had bought Raven Hall, and whose flamboyance and eccentricity extended to a terraced garden planted with iron trees! A compulsive gambler, the doctor eventually staked his mansion on a race between two lice. His bug finished a poor second, and in 1895 the entire estate was acquired by a group of ambitious businessmen who intended to transform the barren headland into a tourist resort. Some roads and villas were built before bankruptcy stifled the plans. The thistled plots and the hall, now a prestige hotel, remain, a tumble-weed dream, mourning the city exodus that never came.

From Ravenscar there are two equally attractive routes to Robin Hood's Bay. On the ebb, the first takes a littoral bee-line avoiding the deep ravines of Stoupe and Mill Becks. The second initially follows the old railway, passing Brickyards Alum Quarry before joining the cliffs. We took the panoramic highroad, encouraged at every step by the lure of our destination — Robin Hood's Bay, for me the most enchanting seaside town in all England, tottering on the edge, a pugnacious Tom Thumb of a town which has suffered for its impudence over the years by successive cliff falls.

Even outlaws need a holiday sometimes, and legend suggests that the eponymous merry man was a regular visitor to the town, practising his skills with the longbow at a place on the adjacent moors still known as Robin Hood's Butts.

For many years Bay Town, as it came to be known, reaped a considerable harvest from smuggling and from fishing, hosting a fleet of over 170 sailing ships owned by local families. Writing in 1892 John Leyland describes the scene... 'The salt, seafaring character rests upon the whole of Bay Town. You may peep in at the open cottage doors, and the narrow interiors will remind you, with their nooks and corners and lockers of what the cabins of old whalers must have been; and the Robin Hood's Bay men had their shares in the operations of the Whitby whaling fleet. Fishing nets and blue jerseys hang from the balconies, and the windows are gay with flowers as the fisherman loves them — and every speck of paint is bright and clean, and there are white curtains at the windows as the Yorkshire housewife loves them too. Rosy-faced lasses stand at the door, and you will hear as you pass the rattling of vessels within as the mother is making ready the meal — a brown-faced, plump, hardy 'throddy body' most likely, as in some parts of Yorkshire they call such a one'.

A tourist haul supports the modern economy, and they come in summer droves, instant converts to the organic architectural style, each cottage snuggling its red tiled neighbour, the crannied whole crowding on every precipitous yard of the stream worn cleft, creating intimacy on an intensely human scale. You may wander along the cobbled maze, finding The Dock, Flagstaff Steps, Jim Bell's Stile and Tyson's Row, inspecting restored cottages — 'Brigantine', 'The Mariners' and 'Seacroft', and if blessed like me you may sling your hammock in a cottage room disdainful of posh hotels and their hedonistic stars. No low beam bumping there. No toasting chilblains. No pykelet feasts. No creepy tales making huddlers of full grown men when the salt-lick vampire taps the pane.

I have stayed in Robin Hood's Bay on many occasions. A workmate's property, willed by a benevolent aunt, is my favourite roost. It consists of 3 stacked rooms decorated in re-emerging 1930's style, a detached kitchen across the alley (alacrity with a frying pan ensures a hot breakfast) and a coal-hole stuffed withold nets, fuel and fish boxes. Wall pinned by the roar in the parlour grate you can blister in patent leather chairs of some pedigree (they were bought from Scarborough, as a job lot from Charles Laughton's famous Pavilion Hotel before demolition), whilst boot-tapping to 80rpm records scratched by an ancient phonograph. To give you some idea of the cottage repertoire, a standard refrain is Mr. Izzy Rubenstein...

'Mr. Izzy Rubenstein who was very old,
One day playing titsy-bing he caught a nasty cold,
His great-great grandson wrapped him up,
And put him into bed,
The lawyer called next morning,
And this is what he said.
Is Mr. Izzy ill, is he, is he?
Has he caught a chill, has he, has he?
Will he make a will, will he will he? ...'

Must remember never to play titsy-bing without wearing my liberty bodice, a garment much appreciated upon concluding an evening's crooning and levering limbs from the said blaze. The rest of the pile is unheated and a dive for the eiderdown, undressing once the hypothermic pain subsides, is commended. Escapee water bottles have been known to freeze solid in that establishment.

Drat! The ice-palace was hosting an eskimo convention. We had to book into the centrally heated Bay Hotel, an inter-tidal hostelry offering impromptu sea-showers whilst contemplating one's dangly bits. I was enthroned until the wave struck and poured through the open window. Curtains, toilet paper and ankled trousers did little to absorb the pool and business was adjourned until I found the ladies.

We had our meal and relaxed by the open fire, transfixed in metaphysical gaze, one stare probing the coals, the other eyeing the surf beyond the bulwark wall. Dog-tired we went aloft to our beds watching the fingering phosphorescence rush even higher up the slipway. Years ago the prow of a shipwreck breached this very room. We listened to the scour and wondered, reassured by an omnipotence beyond the realm of man.

In atrocious weather on the 18th January 1881, the brig *Visitor* foundered in Robin Hood's Bay. High seas prevented the local lifeboat from launching, and in desperation, the Whitby craft was summoned overland, and hauled through 7 feet snowdrifts by over 200 men and 18 horses. A gang of Bay Town men battled up the hill to meet the boat, and two hours after leaving Whitby it was launched and the crew of the *Visitor* were saved. The feat is commemorated by a plaque at the top of the infamous bank which we rounded, pen-pushers wheezing like bronchial donkeys. It would be a long haul today even without the snow.

On leaving Robin Hood's Bay we were immersed in mist, cussing the contrary English weather. Neither hot nor cold it draws out the sap, wetness waxing underarm, spine-fast vests staunching tides of BO, that fetid halo, which, augmented by several days tramping, diverts passing vessels on a wide beam. Formative years as batchelors have robbed us of nasal sensitivity. Mere men, we failed to˙ bring adequate changes of clothing or washing powder. For our omissions we were chastised.

On schedule we rendezvoused with our wives, two Persil piranhas who can strip your clothes for the tub in five seconds. Taking delivery of my freshly starched son, we escaped. The arch-laundresses were sent on ahead to scout for diggings.

Luxurious turf energizes the hooves on the next nine miles to Whitby. Threading between a terrace and its parcelled gardens overlooking the bay, the path leads to the National Trust's Rocket Post Field and the first hurdle on a Grand National course of stiles. Tom clipped the second and yelled, reminded he was a boy. Was I expecting too much of the colt, a mere 5 year old? Chewing on an analgesic chocolate egg he dismissed my parental doubts with a gallop.

The diminutive Rain Dale, surely the tiniest dale in the whole of Yorkshire, debouches a stream over the vast shaly amphitheatre of cliff near Clock Case Nab. We climbed the peak following the bootee tracks, marvelling at the vigour of young limbs. Fuelled by the joys of the open track and prescription Smarties (the ¼lb of eggs lasted but a mile) our guest hiker romped along unbridled, a rousing example to those atrophied, coddled infants of the TV sect.

We found a dead shrew (a carefully pocketed trophy for mummy!), and a pair of stone gate posts, one marked by smugglers with their initials, and a cross and an arrow pointing to a secretive landfall at Pursglove Stye Batts. And then came the view of distant Whitby, as intriguing a land-fall as could be found this side of Treasure Island.

Vying with York as Yorkshire's most famous town, Whitby owes much of its international prominence to a Tyke who christened landfalls the world over. From Mount Cook in New Zealand to Cape Prince of Wales in Alaska, Captain James Cook is acknowledged as the greated combined seaman, explorer, navigator and cartographer of all time.

Cook was born of humble farming stock in 1728 in the obscure village of Marton-in-Cleveland. After a sparse education followed by a brief stint at the plough, the 17 year old Cook left home to take up a position as a grocers and haberdasher's assistant in the thriving fishing village of Staithes. An impressionable and an adventurous youth, he fell under the spell of the sea, deserting his counter for a Whitby apprenticeship under the eye of ship owner John Walker. An eager salt, Cook soon learned his trade aboard shallow draughted colliers,

NEAR CLOCK CASE NAB ... author and freshly starched son.

GRAPE LANE ... Cook's spy-glass berth.

sturdy, stubby little ships, whose practicalities were to prove indispensable in the voyages of discovery yet to come.

Cook joined the Royal Navy in 1755. Within 3 years he had been elevated to the rank of Captain aboard the *Pembroke*, a 64 gun warship deployed against the French. Following sterling service in the siege of Quebec, he went on to chart the St. Lawrence River and the Gulf of Newfoundland. The culmination of his lifetime's ambition came in 1768.

Commissioned by the Admiralty, Cook embarked for the South Seas in a converted Whitby collier, the *Endeavour*, ostensibly on an astronomical mission to observe the transit of Venus. His real goals were the discovery of the illusory southern continent and the expansion of British interests in the Pacific.

With exceptional navigational and cartographical skills, Cook explored the northern coast of Australia, circumnavigated New Zealand and left a string of island discoveries in his wake. A second equally successful expedition aboard the *Resolution*, accompanied by a sister ship *Adventure*, set sail in 1772, adding Christmas and the Hawaiian islands to the expanding science of geography. Four years later Cook embarked on an ill-fated quest for the North-West Passage. He died at the hands of Hawaiian natives and was buried at sea.

The sea off Whitby is shepherded by a lighthouse, impeccably attired in a snow-white cap and glossy black chimneys, and by the Whitby 'Mad Bull', a squat fog-station wearing an outsize bow-tie horn. Thankfully it was a clear day, and we passed by with ear-drums intact, stopping to observe the submarine form of Black Nab, 'decks awash', and Saltwick Nab, a smooth, shaly excrescence devoid of life, reminiscent of the eyesore slag heaps of South Yorkshire. At last we came within view of the most stirring ruin along the entire coast.

Whitby's jagged crown is visible for miles. Smashed by invading Danes and Vikings, bled dry by Henry VIII, and like Scarborough, blasted by Kaiser Bill, even in dignified ruination Whitby Abbey is impressive. Founded by the saintly Hilda in 656, the abbey rose to be the 'Westminster of the Northumbrian Kings', a matchless example of medieval art and architecture. It was the venue for the famous Synod of Whitby which ended the controversy surrounding the fixing of Easter, and it was the home of a lay-brother, the ox-herd Caedmon, 'Father of the English Sacred Song'. According to tradition, the tuneless Caedmon was asleep in charge of the oxen whilst his fellow brothers sang. He dreamt a celestial presence prompting him to sing 'Alas I cannot', he replied. The angel touched his lips urging him to voice the wonder of creation. This he did, recalling the lyric upon wakening. Elected to the priesthood, Caedmon went on to translate the scriptures into Northumbrian verse. He died eulogised by the Venerable Bede, 'Sweet and humble was his poetry; no trivial or vain song came from his lips. Others after him strove to compose religious poems, but none could vie with him, for he learned the art of poetry not from man nor of men but from God'.

Caedmon is remembered by an elegant cross beside the abbey grounds. Squabs of a poetical feather we doffed our caps at the shrine and entered the glebe of St. Mary's.

A sight for salt-caked eyes, the 12th century church of St. Mary's squats above the town, an ecclesiastical redoubt commanding the twin banks of the Esk, Yorkshire's only salmon river buzzing with trawlers and craft of the leisured class. The interior of the church preserves the evidence of the social demarkation of former days. Private, boxed, elevated pews, emblazoned with faded crests, aspire to monopolise an all levelling God.

The church can be reached by road. By far the more romantic and painstakingly heavenly ascent is via an avalanche of steps leading from Church Street. The guidebooks say there are 199 of the blighters. Having sprinted down and masochistically laboured up again, I reckon there are 208. Whatever the tally, brides who insist on climbing to the ceremony are urged to the

WHITBY ... pot luck.

recuperation of separate beds.

Featured in the escape of Bram Stoker's evil creation Dracula (the vampire is said to have changed into a dog to escape capture) the steps disgorge onto the cobbled Church Street and Sandgate, pricked with yards and alley-ways, and pressed with portholed sailors' cottages and shops, offering meat, fresh fruit, wholefood, pungent, raw and hessian bagged, sumptuous teas, souvenirs and talismans. Salivating on the doorstep of Johnson's Pork Butchers a lycanthrope had me hurrying to the jewellers for a lump of fossilised wood. An antidote to the evil eye, Whitby jet has been used since the Bronze Age for ornamentation and for counteracting witchcraft. Fashionable in the Victorian era, jet reached its popularity during the mourning period for Prince Albert, only to decline with the importation of foreign substitutes after 1870. Today the trade has somewhat revived. I bought a jet crucifix and held it ready.

Church Street led us to a patch of ooze on the Esk's east bank, the site for the curious custom of the Horngarth or Penny Hedge. On Ascension Day each year, a barmy duo stomp about in the mud erecting a symbolic 'hedge' of rammed sticks. These must endure for three successive tides. Decreed by the Abbot of Whitby, the ceremony is in atonement for the murder of a hermit by three noble families in 1159. Tom's impromptu imitations of the ritual were curtailed, conscripted hankies restoring his means of recognition.

We entered Grape Lane passing the riverside house where Cook once lodged. His spy glass berth still scans the immutable business of the Esk, skimmed in Summer by yachting dudes, yet busy yearlong with trawlermen. They have their diesels now and sophisticated radar and echo sounders, but they wear their traditional ganseys with quiet pride, these worthy successors to whaling captains like the famous Scoresby's who brought such wealth to the port in the latter part of the eighteenth century.

We loitered on the swing bridge connecting East and West Cliff, looking upstream past the marina, past the high bridge to the heather-clad moors beyond, then round to the red-tiled roofs, down to the fish quay, onward to the pincer arms of the sea-wall and back in a giddy sweep to the jumble of wynds and ghauts from which we came. Lost in thought I pictured old Whitby and its verandahed taverns where shipmates would sit with a pipe and a cool tankard, looking out to sea while the 'silvery freight' was hauled from the smacks.

'You're late!' bellowed the advance party. Startled, thinking it was the mother-in-law, I instinctively brandished my recent purchase. We were again verbally cuffed and ushered on ahead in the direction of a bath.

The proprietor's nose was diverted as we were dragooned to the soak in a cosy boarding house on East Crescent. The scolds had chosen and prepared well. There was H. and C. in all rooms, complimentary soap and towels, good food and ale, and sweet, fresh clothes. Regular Narcissi we felt like a night on the town.

After our meal under a Grimshaw sky, we emerged with camera and tripod seeking to capture the fantasy of shadow and silhouette. The boats were nudged and hawsered, their rested hulls webbed in spars and rigging. The filimented Esk was flecked with nesting birds and all around the high penumbra of cliffs compelled the curfewed night. Bathed in moonlight, disturbed only by the delayed click of the shutter, we steeped in tranquillity, devoting the final frames to Cook's monument on West Cliff. Inspired, a young lad could bide there on a night like that, setting his jib for the stars, aspiring to the great man's own achievements ...'I who had ambition not only to go farther than anyone had gone before, but as far as it was possible for man to go'.

Popping ale buds called us to the diggings bar. It was unblooded save for wet runs by the proprietor, a generous Geordie who served the first commercial drinks free. Deep in the flaps of our underpants, embarrassed denizens of the chrysalis purse stirred as the chilling story of the house unfolded. Peradventure, we had been billeted in a house alleged by our host to have been the setting for part of the dread story of Dracula. 'I usually airs the tale when my guests are departing' said he, producing a dog-eared volume, 'but you look like a couple of lads with plenty of neck'. The recitation began...

'Though the front of our part of the Crescent was in shadow, everything could be well seen — I threw a glance up at our window, and saw Lucy's head leaning out ... There distinctively was Lucy with her head lying up against the side of the window-sill and her eyes shut. She was fast asleep, and by her, seated on the window-sill was something that looked like a full size bird' (him!) ...'as I came into the room she was moving back to her bed, fast asleep and breathing heavily; she was holding her hand to her throat as though to protect it from cold...'

SCARBOROUGH ... take-away meals.

HAYBURN WYKE ... skeleton staffs.

LUNCHBREAK ... please return my hat.

Whitby
Staithes
Saltburn

I awoke to the raucous scream of gulls — the caped avenger! Agh! I checked the carotids for punctures. Phew! The veins were unmolested, so I skipped downstairs and sunk my teeth into breakfast.

The morning was bright with a skin-shearing frost. For the first time in years, the flaps of my deer-stalker were pressed into service. Eskimo clad, Tom enveloped more air than an airship.

With our newly purchased football we headed for Whitby sands. Five kicks and the game was called off and I had to carry the blessed thing. I spent the rest of the day looking like Quasimodo.

We moved on below a £3 million cliff stabilisation scheme, stopping to play noughts and crosses in the sand. Then we splashed in the tide all the way to Sandsend. Tom had his wellies; I had colander boots. If this book sells a few copies I have resolved to buy myself a pair of those Italian jobs with real leather laces. Perhaps royalties could fund matching socks as well?

Socks were the problem. Sat in front of the blazing fire in the lounge of the White Harte, my size 7 defoliants preserved a "cordon sanitaire". Shown the toilet door I consigned the contaminants to the flush and returned in borrowed hose to my pint and Sunday lunch.

Thank the Lord for good old English pubs. Since they began, once again, to offer traditional fayre their popularity has soared. Still, I have cursed them in the past. When I first began walking, it was always a scramble to get to the wickets before closing time. Leaving my laggardly chums behind, I have often charged pell-mell off some dessicated moor in a futile attempt to secure the beers, draping my loofahed tongue across the bar as a tormentor yelled 'Time!' Nowadays I can amble, knowing the licensing laws are, in theory, more relaxed.

Aye, licensed victuallers they were sometimes called, and that was a term that forever confused. The only victuals that were available to companion my drinks were pickled eggs or 'growlers', once lifeless concoctions of pork and pastry, that when fresh could induce the quivers. 'I likes to nibble a little hole in t'crust first. Then I shoves me tongue inside and waggles it about in't succulent juices. Then I gets me lips round't job and sucks and burrows into t'meat and rolls them pieces round me gob...' A fine eulogy to the ultimate home for salmonella.

We waddled from the bar to the sands, relaxing briefly before crossing East Row Beck. We had planned to wander into the beautiful Mulgrave Woods, a detour of some 4 miles, to view a ruined castle and the Wizard's Glen, but time was of the essence and we shoved off for Staithes, minus our wives and Tom who bo-hooed all the way to school.

Crossing Sandsend Beck we entered the old railway yard, now smothered by a 'pay and display' car park. I scoff. Freedom of the road? What myth. The need for economies axed our railways, spawning the proliferation of those all congesting hogs, mass produced, yet paradoxically customised; flaunting their heraldic marques and caudal ironing boards, boasting injection this, turbo that, squeezing like frantic maggots into any recess that will take four wheels. For my sins I was once a car parks' supervisor. Dusting off the memories I passed the line of coin bearers waiting at the machine, thanking providence for a fine pair of legs.

The path follows the track of the redundant line,

leading to a ruddled moonscape of old quarries, which, from the early 17th, to the late 19th century, produced alum in vast quantities. For decades, the Yorkshire coast supplied virtually the entire English market, disfiguring and denuding the landscape, leaving dereliction on a massive scale. Spoilation of this planet is as old as the hills.

Used in medicine, tanning and as a fixing agent for dyes, alum was a difficult substance to extract, calling for the mixing of the shales with rotten seaweed boiled in urine. Oceans of the liquid were shipped from the large towns. I had always wondered what the piggy bank calibrations on my heirloom chamber pot were for. Parsimony, it seems, runs in the family.

Not a blade of grass challenges the sterility of Kettleness, yet moving a few yards inland, we found the greening of a railway cutting almost complete, trees, scrub, gorse, honeysuckle and palettes of Spring flowers gladdening the slopes. We followed the path which aims straight for the tunnel, burrowing for over a mile to Kettleness village. A danger sign warning of roof falls repelled probing eyes.

The path climbed, wriggling under a gnarled and contorted tree, choked by ivy but clinging to precious life. We made the top, enjoying long distance views of Lythe church. Then the Weather Master thundered 'Fore! Hail Caesar!' We cowered until the hailstorm and the headaches subsided.

A short distance from the hamlet of Kettleness we discovered the site of a Roman signal station built in the 4th century to survey 'Dunus Sinus' bay, where the legions had a landing place. Raiders sacked the station after a brief history of only two or three decades, leaving, amongst the ruins, the body of a man, his throat ripped out by a large dog. Grappling skeletons vividly etched the tale.

Taking a detour past Goldsborough, we next came to the modern ruins of a church in the fields above Kettleness. Built in 1872, St. John the Baptist's has been stripped and left to moulder like a sister relic, the farmstead of Scratch Alley, a gaunt roofless building, that, given early retirement, I could redeem with relish. Yes, how I would like to sling my pen, purging my life of the abstract, the theoretic, the conceptual, the grindingly bureaucratic, ridding my days forever of reports, minutes memos, circulars and those endless meetings that produce enough hot air to fuel a squadron of Zeppelins. If I wrote a best-seller I would chuck everything for a bag of tools and blistered hands. Keep on scribbling my boy.

What a vast railway station for such an insignificant place. But quiet resignation has not always been the norm in Kettleness. The alum industry once ensured a Sunday congregation and a brief prosperity that led to doom.

One night in December 1829 the inhabitants of the old village awoke to the sound of subterranean groans. Fearing subsidence they evacuated to the safety of a schooner anchored in the bay. A few hours later the entire village dropped into the sea.

A handful of successor dwellings and the railway station inherit the cliff top shales. The pride of the LNER is today packed to the ceiling with bunks, a three-tiered assault course for cubs and scouts who billet here each Summer.

Following the curving railway track above the bay, we greeted bonny Runswick — with mile long sands the perfect place for loafing. Packed higgledy piggledy into the cliff side, eaves snuggling eaves, (the thicket of chimney pots must ease the lot of Santa), bright with fresh licked paint, brasses, figure heads and flowers, Runswick smiles at the sea as though they were bosom pals. The reality is somewhat different. Like neighbouring Kettleness, over the centuries, Runswick has suffered from erosion. In 1682 the entire village, excepting one house, 'went to sea'. It is recalled that a drinking party was toasting a dear-departed in the local inn. A latecomer

BLACK NAB ... decks awash.

STAITHES ... they came for the toffee apples.

RUNSWICK BAY ... the thicket of chimney pots eases the lot of Santa.

stumbled on the threshold. Usually associating his clumsiness with the return journey he blinked in puzzlement, examining his boots, the doorstep and finally the path which had disappeared into a yawning chasm. Rousing his chums he led the hasty flight through the back door to raise the alarm. By prodigious efforts all the villagers were saved.

The gradient into the village had us sprinting, packs-a-thumping, to the beach. We rested awhile on the sea-wall and wandered, avoiding the temptation of the Royal Hotel. On nooky paths and stairways we threaded between cottages fixed like martens' nests to the cliff. What architectural idiosyncrasy. What fun. We noticed the dapper Runswick Stores set on a bogey. 'And look at that listed building', chirped my long silent chum (we had not passed a church organ for miles and he felt grumpy). Yes, the shack did list. It was canted, capsized, its six square feet occupied almost entirely by an old salt's cot.

Before we left Runswick we fell into conversation with a local man, busily cropping his sward with garden shears. He solved a lifetime's mystery.

As bare arsed lads we were chided by our mums with the phrase "You'll catch kink-cough in your bums". What in tarnation was kink-cough and would it hurt? Well, apparently, there were, explained the gardener, pointing and nearly cleaving off my nose, several sea caves in the locality. In one, known as Hob Holes, lived a goblin reputed to have the power of curing whooping cough. Leading afflicted children, mums would resort to the cave and recite the words:-

Hob-hole Hob!
Ma bairn's getten t'kink-cough:
Tak't off — tak't off!'

So now we know. Runswick was, he went on, a real hive of superstition. Before the return of the fleet in the old days, expectant fishwives would slaughter a number of cats for good luck, and in bad weather, village children would dance around a cliff top fire chanting:-

'Souther wind, souther,
And blow father home to my mother.'

'Reminds me of one of my own schoolboy superstitions', said I. "Condemned to six of the best I would run a magical tile, in reality a bathroom reject, across the palm. On one occasion the 'cane-break' worked!"

Idle banter was delaying the march to Staithes. We thanked our helpful friend and pondered yet another Eiger wall.

'Half a league, half a league, half a league onward'. I led the way to Runswick Bank Top and the regained Cleveland Way.

Slogging along 'Wilfs Way', with hardly a care for Coble Dump or Lingrow Knock reef, we made Port Mulgrave within the hour. And yet again, down we went, zig-zagging hundreds of feet to a real dump, a man made affair, effluvial and rusting, abandoned to the keel-worn boats of lobster fishermen since its iron ore terminal closed in the 1920's. A two mile long tunnel linked the bay with Grinkle Mines near Daleshouse south of Staithes. The ore was carried on a narrow gauge railway for shipment by coaster to the furnaces of Jarrow. Since closure the quay has foundered and the tunnel has been bricked up, leaving a sulking destitution; a beach littered with twisted metal, sparkless engines amber with age, stagnant pools, discarded bottles and tins and a pair of goats sculking round a tumble of huts.

Alfred J. Brown in his book "Fair North Riding" recommends Mulgrave for a dip. If you fancy contusions, grazes or worse, dive in, and leave your clothes unattended. They could end up like my map...goat fodder. 'Take a photograph quickly' I implored. My photographer was still smarting from the escapade with his horned subject in Ringborough. Cautiously he produced a telephoto lens that doubled as a jousting lance. He screwed and fiddled and finally took the picture, sadly missing the opportunity for supplying evidence for my insurance claim.

Dragging our tired pins over the final two miles to

SKINNINGROVE ... how sweet was my valley.

HUMMERSEA ... an orchid peeping.

SALTBURN ... peering out.

Staithes we came within view of the new Low Boulby potash mine which stains the horizon with a sickly plume of smoke. The rape goes on.

We entered Staithes village and examined the huddle of cottages, but the architectural assessment had to wait. We were jiggered. We needed a bed for the night: or rather two beds.

His Nibs must want me to succeed with this book, for why else would He contrive yet another berth at a house with literary connections. We stood at the portals of St. Martin's Lodge in High Street and knocked. The landlady appeared and instilled us with the fear of Bobby George. Assuming that we had arrived by car, she immediately voiced the pains of illegal parking. 'He'll have your tyres off will Bobby George. He's a bugger is Bobby George'.

I realised that the lady was describing a member of the constabulary and not some kleptomaniac with an obsession for rubber. 'No, oh no, we've walked missis. We've walked from Sandsend'. The laser eyes transfixed our boots. We removed them without a peep and followed her upstairs to a tastefully decorated and furnished garret room with apexed, very low, matt-black beams. I wonder if one of the previous occupants of the room, the famous James Herriot used margarine on his lumps! The budding author is said to have stayed there on his honeymoon. Bet he never wore socks in bed.

We slumped and studied the rafters. 'I've just realised something' said a tired voice. 'There is no door on this room. If some rampant woman wanted to get in during the night we would have no protection but your socks'.

'Vitenery' is not the only celebrity to have graced the lodge. It was formerly owned by Marie M. Lowden, the 'Toffee Lady of Staithes'. Her book 'Behind the Scenes in Yorkshire' recalls some of the history of what became known as the 'Toffee Crackle House'. Following the premature death of her husband, Mrs. Lowden was left in dire financial straits. She takes up the story... 'I was left a widow with a mortgage and all the renovation bills to be paid. Guests started coming, and that *did* help. Then my youngest daughter had the idea of making and selling toffee apples to the crowds of visitors who came during the summer months from all over the world in turbans, fez, saris, Africans in colourful Western garb, and they all bought our toffee apples. Then some visitors said they preferred the toffee which dripped from the apples, so we sold the toffee itself. And within nine years of my husband's death, the house and all the bills were paid for'.

Nearing her eighties, Mrs. Lowden moved to more manageable accommodation in 1982. The 'Toffee Crackle' tag lingers on.

The recuperative powers of cold water. A quick 'swill' and we were ready for the night shift. 'I'll phone the 'Royal George' and tell him I'm sending two of my boys over for dinner', said the landlady. 'Steaks be alright?'

Six-thirty and the pub was shut. Hunger marked time while we explored. Lodged in a dislocation of the rock, a ravel of narrow pathways and streets, anchored, tier upon tier in the sinews of its beck, Staithes recoils from the sea. Cook wanted to confront it.

On that chill night, floating above the chimney pots, coughing on the muck from a dozen smoking chimneys, peering down into a grey huddled bowl, I pondered the postcard image and the reality of an, in parts, unkempt and degenerating village, suffering, despite the influx of seasonal visitors, the effects of recession. And I thought about the olden times, when none of us ventured further than the garden gate, when rheumy Staithes drooped with nets and when insularity and isolation set ambitions charting warmer climes. Is it any wonder that Cook's South Seas beckoned?

On we went, aleward, a jumble of steps leading us to a strangely inscribed tablet set into a wall. "This covert was planted in memory of Spadger, 1st Baron Sparrow, the herod of a hundred fights. Died March 1901" What covert

STAITHES ... the Cod and Lobster under the lash.

and who was Spadger? We never found out.

The maze brought us back to narrow High Street, where argumentative cars and lorries have left their marks. High Street is home to a sprinkling of shops, some dilapidated and empty, others modern and functional, and one, a triumphant demonstration of the art of squeezing a quart into a pint pot. It brings an unaccustomed veracity to the term 'general store' and it kept our attention until opening time. There are medicines and books, there are tins and toy trucks and sweets by the jostling jar. There are hammers and saws, pincers with claws, a spade and a 42″ bra. Aye, I could have rambled poetical about that store, had I not been deflected by a laconic passer-by. 'If they haven't got it' (he spat out the words) 'it's not worth having'. We walked on to the sea.

If 'Old Ma Staithes' hides from the waves, with an impudent toe, her beery bairn double-dares them. Perched on the slipway wall, risking her barrels to the frequent lash, the Cod and Lobster has long since been the haunt of fishermen after a hard day; but early doors and we found not a gansey in sight, but crowds of fashionable young men clamouring around a juke-box. We slinked to a corner by the fire with other old momentoes — dozens of photographs showing the bowsprit pub and a gallery of grizzled boatmen and ladies dressed in the famous Staithes bonnets.

What would Cook's successors have made of our fellow customers with their severely cropped heads? The tonsorial fashions of today would, I am sure, have pleased the surgeon/barbers of those convict ships just decades down the line.

We hurried to the George for our meal and the maul accomplished, we preened and relaxed with a pint. A dog idled in, jumped up on the couch, and shuffled towards an old lady who was skirmishing with a dish of shell-on prawns. 'You've pinched his seat', I said jokingly. 'Huh' she rasped between dismembering plucks. 'You cannot reserve places here my man: it's bums that bag seats'.

Within seconds there were no seats left and we were hemmed in by a volcanic ring, a duo of pipe smokers stoking their miniature Vesuvius's which spewed magma all over a gentleman's chocolate pud. We retreated under the smoke screen and eyes watering coughed our way to the bar for a final drink. We drank and decided to drink again, remembering the low beams and ordering a round of anaesthetic rums.

We awoke and dressed, but not a mouse stirred. The frying pan was cold. Where was the flower of English fryers? She was a-bed.

There followed an enforced constitutional, after which we returned to the sizzle of bacon and arraignment at the court of the electronic windbag. Force-fed television at that hour in the morning gives me bilge-ache. Such is the insatiable appetite of the masses, however, that the Nips, I understand, are working on a 24 hour coverage miniset implant to replace redundant brain cells. Risking indigestion we bolted our food and headed into the mist.

My first act, one that later in the day was to imperil our chances of sleeping on anything other than a park bench, was to pose for an apt front cover photograph. Remembering the escapade with the goats, the boot was truly on the other foot, and vengeful lens had me clarting around in the Staithes beck, grappling oily strands. Was it worth a tin of Swarfega, an ounce of wire wool and skin grafts? No! See what that meddling publisher chose!

Saltburn

Redcar

Middlesbrough

Land of cliffs — Cleveland. Now I know why it is so called. What climbs! What cleavage! For dodo's like me parachutes should be worn over the next few miles.

Leaving Staithes, ignoring the faecal plume of Low Boulby mine, we broached strands of pernicious bracken that contest the cliff-top sod of Lingberry Hill with heather. And not for the first time, we lost the path, a translucent aquamarine sea disclosing its girdle of reefs, luring us to the foot of the highest cliffs in England.

Boulby Cliffs disguise their 660 feet in bouldered graduation. Exploitation for building materials, iron-stone, alum and jet has left dunes of barren shales, shattered rocks, moss lined adits, crumbling buildings, and a pair of tiered pyramids built of Aztec stone —giant vats used for the soaking of alum.

We ascended, labouring over the debris, which is said to occasionally catch fire, the result of decomposition and spontaneous combustion or iron sulphide leeching from unstable shales. Ragged from the long miles, my boots were destined for the pyre at stride's end, but I had intended to kick them off first and the thought of roasted chilblains did nothing for my jangled nerves.

I must admit it. I can cope with instinctive flight from bulls but the slow thumb-screw grip of vertigo as we lumbered ever higher made my heart pound. For the first time on my walk I was scared.

I am normally the most rational of blokes — by profession a project planner, a logician — so why does mounting panic set in when I am faced with the Tarpeian wall?

In my dash to make the top, I rushed, forgetting to reconnoitre the route and to test hand and foot holds. As a complete contrast, the old goat beside me, wondering what all the fuss was about, even had time to shoot a couple of frames at a passing blue-winged butterfly. How I envied those wings. Still, who needs flight with celestial Sherpas like my guardian angel. He dragged me over the lip, my face aglow like the fiery stacks of distant Tees.

Within half a mile my dander was raised again. I picked up a stick to clobber two man-eating geese that defend Warren Cottages. 'They're all gob', said a pinafored miss, leading us to a peep of orchids above Hummersea Beach.

Over the years I have seen my foul share of despoilation. My childhood playground in East Leeds was the Bank, a desolation of abandoned back-to-back houses, warehouses, a bombed out school and fly-tipping galore. Even the memories of that rat infested slum could ill prepare me for what I saw next — from the cliffs, a rust coloured worm, neoned, fluorescent bright — the Kilton Beck whose valley has been degraded by decades of industrialisation from Paradise to something resembling an Andean shanty town.

Examine the benign industrialisation at Port Sunlight and Saltaire, erected in the days even before planning controls. Then wince at Skinningrove. The architect for this town, working to the whiphand of skinflint clients, produced little more than perfunctory scribble, a mean design for mean rigid rows of parallel terraced houses that choke the valley floor. Modern housing continues the drab theme. In redemption, higher up the slopes, are carefully tended lines of prize leeks and brightly painted pigeon lofts. On the crests of the hills, inevitable factories spill unmentionable filth.

We dropped down to take a cautious peep, passing rows of scruffy fishermen's huts to a bridge over pure

BOULBY CLIFFS ...
Aztec stone alum vats.

UNDER WARSETT HILL ...
definitely not a church!

pollutant. Here displayed is the most redundant sign along the east coast, warning the public of the dangers of eating contaminated shell-fish.

Thinking about eating, we sought out a hostelry, arriving at the bizarre Timm's Coffee House on New Company Row. As you know, ordinarily we remove our boots before entering such places but this was no ordinary coffee house. A veritable House of Shaws, its front door smashed and boarded up, its stonework fractured and subsided, and its cracked windows variously repaired with place-mats and assorted cardboard, it served neither coffee nor food, my request for sandwiches meeting with a reaction of mirthful incredulity. Sandwiches! I might as well have asked for oysters! Crisps were good enough for the likes of us, and crisps is what we got, washed down with strong ale.

After 'lunch' we should have continued a little way up the road to visit the Tom Leonard Mining Museum. Still hungry we were in no mood for the history of the ironstone industry, so we stayed put, refilled our pots and had a lively debate about the current vogue for industrial museums. Forget the appalling working conditions and wages. Forget the exploitation of infant workers, the injuries and the fatalities. Ignore the continuing blight on the environment — there is money to be made, so let's create an industrial museum. If Old Nick himself could get a grant from British Gas, he too could join the club with a collection of bellows and toasting forks!

If only Skinningrove could turn back the clock it would have no need for contrived attractions. Netted in 1535 a creature brought instant fame to the town. Well authenticated, it was displayed in a hut and fed on raw fish and was described thus:-

'Instead of Voyce he shreaked and shewed himself courteous to such as flocked farre and near to visit him; fayre Maydes were welcomest Guests to his harbour whome he woulde beholde with a very earneste countenaynce as if his plegmaticke Breaste had been touched with a sparke of love.'

Imagine the media and tourist invasions today. The attraction would leave Copenhagen's symbol high and dry. Yes I would skip lunch anyday to see a merman.

Is it an arm of the prison wall bristling with warning notices and barbed wire? No, it is Skinningrove Jetty built for the shipment of ore to the blast furnaces of the Tyne and Tees. The local mines finally closed in 1958 abandoning that slab of concrete to the years.

Stumbling over a clinkered track, we jumped from that jetty onto Cattersty Sands. Given blinkers we could well have landed on a tropical isle. Such golden grains, so soft and duney, ideal for sunbathing, and if a flaccidity of condoms was anything to go by, for parallel pursuits.

We pressed on and for the second time that day we were deflected, leaving the Cleveland Way, to inspect a churchy looking ruin. Beside a railway line under Warsett Hill, the brick-built structure is, on closer inspection, definitely not a church... but what is it? The evidence of a vaulted shaft, and a tower which obviously housed a huge revolving drum, point to an engine-house for ore separation? Mysteriously, the building is not marked on the OS map, (a military installation?) although the notation 'air shaft' shown slightly above the 325' contour line would indicate the presence of a long tunnel. Very interesting 'mon ami'. 'Clouseau!' I was rudely interrupted. 'I'm ravenous. Get a move on!'

Victuals first; digs later; that was the plan. But oh the schemes of mice and men. Saltburn was shut. And so like ragged Legionnaires, we roamed the streets looking for accommodation. An appetising patch of nasturtiums led us up a garden path to Noble House. We knocked. We pressed the bell. 'Noble? No bell', said my side-kick after five depressing minutes.

The search led us on to Emerald Street, to the Blue

Rose Guest House and a reviving pot of sweet, galvanic tea. You hear tales of the salubrious properties of this beverage. Short of raising the dead it is good for all ills. Two cups each and a shared plate of dunked Garibaldi's and we were rejuvenated. Next came the shower, a device I have learnt something about on my travels. A fumbler with high-tech, I now always send my companions into the dousing room first. There is an eccentricity, an unfathomable irascibility about showers. Their instructions for use could well be written in Hebrew as far as I am concerned. I either end up with burns or with a Bird's eye glaze, or at least I did until I had such guinea pig friends.

Pork was not on the menu. Still, I could eat fish until the sea-cows come home. Perhaps I have merman ancestors? Enough babble! At last we had found somewhere to dine, and we tucked in at the admirable Ship Inn in Old Saltburn. Over our jugs we read the history of the place.

Beginning as the site of a hermitage around 1215, picturesque Old Saltburn relied on fishing, seal catching and smuggling until the railway came in 1860. Apart from the Ship, the haunt of the notorious smuggler John Andrews, there is little left of the original settlement, having been eclipsed by the Victorian development of the cliff in the decade after 1860. Enjoying a fine elevated position overlooking 5 miles of excellent beach and the delightful valley of the Skelton Beck, Saltburn-by-the-Sea retains its ordered charm, echoed in rows of rectory style houses and in elegant public buildings like the railway station and the former Zetland Hotel now converted to flats.

Our jugs were empty, so we left for the Blue Rose, trotting smartly past the old mortuary of 1881. You will note that every convenience is provided for walkers in Saltburn.

We were up at 'sparrow fart' to use a colloquial expression. The limey Luftwaffe had hardly had chance to quit the roost as we took the grand tour beginning at the 'funiculee! funicular!' The sun was shining. What a lovely morning for a song.

'That's a bit steep' said I looking over the cliff at the world's oldest hydraulic inclined railway. 'Downright robbery if you ask me', said my pal looking at the tariff board. 'Gravity's a lot cheaper'. I agreed and down we stepped to Saltburn Pier, another stout Victorian creation offering a bracing promenade if you can first run the gauntlet of ear cuffing zaps and lasers. It pays to come early. You cannot feed coin with the switches up and it is so quiet. And it was quiet too on the slipway and the sea-wall, built from stones which originally formed part of the Stockton to Darlington railway, the serenity extending to the lovely Valley Gardens where we discovered another outsize piece of railway memorabilia — the portico of Barnard Castle railway station.

And so to the final proper breakfast on our journey. Tomorrow we would be back to a regimen of muesli and prune juice, so like condemned men we ate a hearty plate of fat, deluged with sugared tea you could have drunk from a trowel.

Over breakfast we chatted with very convivial company — a slim retiring actress (my she could trough!) who had once appeared in the TV series 'Brideshead Revisited', and our estimable landlady who cleared up the enigma of the Blue Rose. To no avail, her father-in-law spent a lifetime attempting to cultivate a blue rose, the quest being continued by her husband, whose ambition is symbolised by their definitive blue sign. Raise your cups. A toast in tea. Success to green fingers and may the greenfly be sparse this year.

On to Redcar, leads pancake beach, eight miles of sand hallowed by the tyre tracks of Malcolm Campbell who twice attempted to break the world land speed record here in the 1920's. Down to the last few coppers, we too were pitted against the clock (British Rail time-pieces

SALTBURN – INCLINED RAILWAY ... gravity is cheaper.

wait for no man) and we left the sands at Marske and trudged in heavy rain along the A1042 into Redcar. You can see ships from the road, lumbering from the estuary heavy with cargo, an inspirational sight that once put a certain Samuel Plimsoll in line for immortality.

Entering Redcar we took shelter, ducking into the RNLI museum, the home of the oldest lifeboat in the world. The venerable Zetland was built in 1800 and saved over 500 lives in 78 years of service, rescuing sailors of all nationalities from the scores of vessels wrecked on Redcar's treacherous rocks and reefs. This Chelsea Pensioner of a boat is surrounded by trophies recording her many feats. In attendant rooms are other interesting exhibits, models, list of wrecks, stuffed fish, a replica fisherman's cottage and portraits of famous lifeboatmen like Plunger Boagey, Laurie Picknett and that anonymous bearded soul whose face has brightened 'Skipper' brand sardine cans for years. Lovingly assembled by volunteers, the exhibitions serve this unique service proud. A displayed tribute from Sir Winston Churchill, for me, says it all; 'A lifeboat, it drives on with a mercy which does not quail in the presence of death, it drives on as a proof, a symbol, a testimony that man is created in the image of God and that valour and virtue have not perished in the British race'. And there's more...

I have referred to the wonderful band of RNLI volunteers, in whose numbers are the indispensable lady-organisers, fund raisers and those who merely 'stand and wait'. A credit to their menfolk, these helpers enhance the institution's already considerable prestige, none more so than RNLI gold medal winner, the jolly and irrepressible Vera Robinson, former chairperson, secretary and treasurer of the local lifeboat association, and author, raconteur and walking encyclopaedia of Redcar life. Meeting Vera at the door we were treated to a selection of anecdotes and songs. The lady hardly drew breath, recalling her younger days, when, before school, children had to fetch their 1d. buckets of seawater up to

the hydropathic hotels for sale, when George Formby made his debut at the 'Arcadia' and when 'Cousin Tom' accompanied on the melodian, sang his famous song on the beach...

'Sunshine Corner-oh it's jolly fine,
It's for children under 99,
All our welcome seats are given free,
Redcar Sunshine Corner is the place for me.'

We giggled at the tune and at the following tale concerning an unusual local street-name. Graffenberg Street is named after a distinguished Austrian physician who once practiced in the town. One morning after a terrible storm, a luckless corpse was found by a fisherman washed up opposite the aforementioned street. Eager to claim his 5 shillings reward, the fisherman proceeded to the police station to record his find. The interrogation went like this. 'Sex?' 'Male'. 'Approximate Age?' '45' 'Where found?' 'Graffenberg Street'. 'Oh, er... Well can you drag him down a bit?' 'I can't spell Graffenberg.'

We saw very little else of Redcar. The racecourse, Locke Parke, the largest indoor funfair in the North-East, and High Street's imposing clock tower erected in 1910 to commemorate King Edward VII, would have to tarry for another day. We had four hours to reach the Tees for our Middlesbrough train.

What a funeral end to an otherwise exhilarating walk. Attempting to find the Tees we were aliens lost in an industrial labyrinth, dwarfed by belching chimneys and pylons, and endangered by intimidating high voltage cables, gas pipes, and a web of railway lines. Whatever became of the Fisherman's Trod which before industrialisation wound its way from creek to lonely creek? Located with the help of a kindly weigh-bridge clerk, it was there still, a mere thread, constricted between factories and flame-licked coking ovens where men in vizors raked to the klaxon sound. Burdened with coils, sheet steel, girders and smoking ingots, slow, almost

MIDDLESBROUGH ... where's the Black Path?

silent shunters hereabouts have caused a number of fatalities to unwary pedestrians, so we were mighty glad of our escort over the rails, onto the locally known Black Path.

The focus of stares by passing drivers, we hurried on with our mouths shut, conscious of endangered health, hardly daring to breath. We passed derelict areas strewn with discarded tons of concrete and metal, past flare-stacks and chimneys trailing sherbet-yellow smoke, past putrid streams, glossy black and pungent with effluent, coughing through poisoned air, to a most extraordinary meeting with a lone, indignant partridge. Eventually we saw the Tees, old Yorkshire's northerly frontier lined with ships and crowned with an iron maiden — the Transporter Bridge, for me, in that present mood, the sole reward for 188 years of exploitation. It is mind-boggling to think that in 1801 Middlesbrough and district consisted of four farmhouses and had a population of only 25.

We have all heard of the town with no name, but a town without a past is a bird of an altogether different feather. The Black Path delivered us to this place, plumb centre, where, draped across the road, was a banner, proclaiming a 'Town without history, important without antiquity — crept out of the Cleveland Hills like a strong invincible serpent'. We would agree with that. It had nearly poisoned us.

Transformed — Arcadia to Vulcan's town in a few short years — the revolution wrought by a handful of men. Notable amongst them was the Quaker industrialist John Pease, a land speculator who, following the extension of the Stockton-Darlington Railway in 1831, recognised the potential of Middlesbrough as a port for the exportation of north country coal. Close on his heels were Henry Bolckow, an emigrant from Mecklenburg, and John Vaughan. Together they created the iron industry, influencing the development of a town described by Gladstone in 1869 as 'the youngest child of England's enterprise, but, if an infant, an infant Hercules'.

Were there rewards from all this development? Built in 1911, there is the impressive Transporter Bridge, the largest of its kind in the world, and other locally produced Meccano sets — the Tyne Bridge, the Menai Bridge, Sydney Harbour Bridge and Denmark's Storstrom Bridge. As for architectural and cultural heritage, apart from the town hall, certain buildings on Queen's Terrace and Zetland Road, and a number of galleries and museums, there is little to warrant a special excursion to the town. But we were there, and we had 57 minutes to spare, just enough time to fly around the Dorman Museum and to enjoy a collection of modern sculptures in the shopping centre. Then apart from one last act, it was pack-up-your-old-kit-bag-time.

I had that one painful duty to perform before we caught the train — to condemn old friends to the pyre. No! My companion had not keeled over at the final frame. Remember? It was those boots. They had been certified dead by a cobbler pal of mine even before we had set out, so you can imagine their condition after so many miles. They were shot. Collecting sticks I reminisced.

Seven years ago I took those daisies off the hands of a park ranger. I had written the £5. I.O.U. on his pot leg. What splendid vehicles they have been — quiet, non-polluting and exceptionally economical. Depth of hard skin suggests they have paced some 10,000 miles, and at one twentieth of a penny per mile I reckon they have been good value.

On some spare land I arranged the pile and lit the match, only at the very last moment pulling the laces and, without blindfolds, committing the boots to the flame. Ghandi had not a finer send off.

And now, my odyssey completed, I shall rest and enjoy a day out in Withernsea on the royalties. But if someone mentions a sequel, it will be a dash to the Army and Navy Stores before this print is dry!

THE END.

Appendix

Some Recommended Accommodation

A tent or canoe-houseboat would work out much cheaper than the following:

Easington
Corner Cottage Guest House
Easington
Nr. Hull
HU12 0TN

Hornsea
Sandhurst Guest House
3 Victoria Avenue
Hornsea

Bridlington
Ivanhoe Guest House
68 New Burlington Road
Bridlington
YO15 3HS

Filey
Lynwood House
50 West Avenue
Filey
YO14 9BE

Carr Naze Hotel
70 Muston Road
Filey
YO14 0AL

Flamborough
Weybourne
North Marine Road
Flamborough
YO15 1LF

The Grange
Bempton Lane
Flamborough
YO15 1AS

Scarborough
Amber Lodge Guest House
17 Trinity Road
Scarborough
YO11 2TD

Red Roofs
42 West Street
Scarborough
YO11 2QR

Scarborough
Mountview Hotel
32 West Street
Scarborough
YO11 2QP

Whitby
Crescent House
6 East Crescent
Whitby
YO21 3HD

The Langley
16 Royal Crescent
Whitby
YO21 3LJ

Robin Hood's Bay
Bay Hotel
The Dock
Robin Hood's Bay

Staithes
St. Martin's Lodge
High Street
Staithes
Cleveland
TS13 5BQ

Saltburn
Blue Rose Guest House
34 Emerald Street
Saltburn-by-the-Sea
Cleveland